K. Bunbury

Letters Written by a Peruvian Princess

Vol. 1

K. Bunbury

Letters Written by a Peruvian Princess
Vol. 1

ISBN/EAN: 9783743358331

Manufactured in Europe, USA, Canada, Australia, Japa

Cover: Foto ©Thomas Meinert / pixelio.de

Manufactured and distributed by brebook publishing software (www.brebook.com)

K. Bunbury

Letters Written by a Peruvian Princess

LETTERS

WRITTEN BY A

PERUVIAN PRINCESS.

A NEW EDITION.

IN TWO VOLUMES.

VOL. I.

DUBLIN:

Printed for WILLIAM COLLES, in Dame-ſtreet;
and RICH. MONCRIEFFE, in Capel-ſtreet.

M.DCC.LXXIV.

LIFE OF

MADAM De GRAFIGNY,

Member of the Academy of Florence.

Taken from different periodical Publications.

MADAM De Grafigny was born in Lorrain, December 12, 1695, and died at Paris, in the 64th year of her age. She was called Frances D'Happoncourt; and was the only daughter of Francis Henry of Iffemburg, lord of Happoncourt, Grieux, &c. lieutenant of the light-horfe; major of the guards to his royal highnefs Leopold I. duke of Lorrain; and governor of Boulay and Larre. Her mother was Margaret de Seaureau, daughter of Anthony de Seaureau, baron of Houdemoure Vandœvre, and firft fteward of the houfhold to the fame duke Leopold. The father of Madam de Grafigny, who by defcent was of the houfe of Iffemburg in Germany, in his younger days ferved in the French army. He was aid de camp to marfhal Bouflers at the fiege of Namur. Lewis the XIV. in recompence for his fervices, made him a gentleman of France, as he was before of Germany; and confirmed all his titles. He afterwards attached himfelf to the court of Lorrain.

His

His daughter was married to Francis Huguet of Grafigny, exempt of the body guards, and chamberlain to the duke of Lorrain. Much did she suffer from the treatment of her husband: and after many years of heroic patience, was juridically separated from him. She had some children by him, who all died young, before their father.

Madam Grafigny was of a grave disposition; her conversation did not display those talents which she had received from nature. A solid judgment, a heart tender and benevolent, and a behaviour affable, uniform and ingenuous, had gained her many friends, a long time before she had any prospect of having literary admirers.

Mademoiselle de Guise coming to Paris to celebrate her nuptials with the duke de Richelieu, brought with her madam de Grafigny; and but for this incident perhaps she would never have seen that city; at least her situation in life by no means gave her reason to think of it: neither had she, nor any of her friends, at that time, the least prospect of the reputation which attended her in that capital. Several persons of wit, who were united into a society, of which she also became a member, insisted on her giving them something for their *Recueil*, which was printed in duodecimo, in the year 1745. The piece which she gave is the most considerable in that collection. It is called, *Nouvelle Espagnole*; *le mauvais exemple produit autant de vertus que de vices* * : The title itself, we see, is a maxim, and the novel is full of them. This little piece was not relished by some of the associates. Madam de Grafigny, piqued at the pleasantries of those gentlemen on her Spanish novel,

* A Spanish novel: bad examples produce as many virtues as vices.

novel, without saying any thing to the society, composed the *Letters of a Peruvian*, which had the greatest success. A short time after she gave the French theatre, Cenie, a piece of five acts in prose, which was received with an applause that has continued to the present day. This play is one of the best we have of the sentimental kind.

La Fille d'Aristide, another comedy in prose, had not, on the representation, the same success with Cenie. It was published after the death of madam Grafigny: they say that the author corrected the last proof on the very day of her death. It is also confidently reported, that the ill success of this piece on the stage, contributed not a little to the disorder of which she died. Madam de Grafigny had that laudable regard for her reputation which is the parent of many talents; a censorious epigram had given her great chagrin; and which she freely acknowledged.

Besides these two printed dramas, madam de Grafigny wrote a little fairy tale of one act, called *Azor*, which was performed at her own apartments; and which she was persuaded not to give to the comedians. She also composed three or four pieces of one act that were represented at Vienna, by the children of the emperor: these are of the simple and moral kind, on account of the august characters who were to be instructed by them.

Their imperial majesties, the emperor, and empress, queen of Hungary and Bohemia, honoured our author with a particular esteem, and made her frequent presents: as did also their royal highnesses prince Charles, and the princess Charlotte of Lorrain, with whom she had moreover the distinguished honour of a literary correspondence.

Madam

Madam de Grafigny left her books to the late M. Guymont de la Touche, author of the modern tragedy of Iphigenia en Tauride, and of the Epistle to Friendship. He enjoyed this donation but little more than a year, for he died himself in the month of February, 1760. She left all her papers to the care of a man of letters; who had been her friend for thirty years; with the liberty of difpofing of them in fuch manner as he thought proper.

We may judge of the genius of madam de Grafigny by her writings, which are in the hands of every one: and of her morals we may judge by her friends, for she had none but those of the greateft merit: and their affliction is her eulogy. The diftinguifhing marks of her character were a fenfibility, and a goodnefs of her heart, fcarcely to be paralleled. Her whole life was one act of beneficence. We know but few particular circumftances relating to it; for she never fpoke of herfelf, and her actions were covered with the veil of fimplicity and modefty. We know in general, indeed, that her life was a continued feries of misfortunes; and doubtlefs it was from thefe that she drew, in part, that amiable and fublime philofophy of the heart, which characterifes her works, and will make them dear to pofterity.

THE

THE

French EDITOR's

ADVERTISEMENT.

IF truth, when it ftrays from probability, ufually lofes it credit in the eye of reafon, it is for a fhort time only ; but, let it contradict prejudice ever fo little, and feldom fhall it find grace before that tribunal.

What then ought not the editor of this work to fear, in prefenting to the public the letters of a young *Peruvian,* whofe ftile and thoughts fo little agree with the mean idea, which an unjuft prejudice has caufed us to form of that nation.

Enriched by the precious fpoils of *Peru,* we ought, at leaft, to regard the inhabitants of that part of the world as a magnificent people ; and the fentiment of refpect is not very remote from the idea of magnificence.

But fo prejudiced are we always in our own favour, that we rate the merit of other nations not only in proportion as their manners imitate ours,

A 4   but

but in proportion as their tongues approach nearer to our idiom. *How can any one be a* Perſian * ?

We deſpiſe the *Indians,* and hardly grant a thinking ſoul to thoſe unhappy people : yet their hiſtory is in every one's hands, and abounds with monuments of the ſagacity of their minds, and the ſolidity of their philoſophy.

The apologiſt of humanity, and of beautiful nature †, has traced the outlines of the *Indian* manners in a dramatic poem, the ſubject of which divides the glory with the execution.

With ſo much light given us into the characters of theſe people, there ſhould ſeem no room to fear that original letters, which only exhibit what we already know of the lively and natural wit of the *Indians,* are in danger of paſſing for a fiction. But hath prejudice any eyes ? There is no ſecurity againſt its judgment, and we ſhould have been careful not to ſubmit this work to it, if its empire had been without bounds.

It ſeems needleſs to give notice, that the firſt letters of *Zilia* were tranſlated by herſelf : every one muſt eaſily judge, that, being compoſed in a language, and traced in a manner equally unknown to us, this collection could never have reached us, if the ſame hand had not writ them over in our tongue.

We

* The tranſlator apprehends this ſentence to be a ſatirical repetition after ſome other *French* author. There were a few ſtrokes marked in the ſame manner in one or two of the letters, which he did not take notice of, as he ſuppoſed they would be unintelligible to the *Engliſh* reader.

† M. de *Voltaire.*

We owe this tranflation to *Zilia's* leifure in her retreat : her complaifance in communicating them to the chevalier *Deterville*, and the permiffion he at laft obtained to keep them, were the means that conveyed them into our hands.

It will eafily be feen, by the faults of grammar and negligence of ftile, that we have been fcrupuloufly careful not to take away any thing of the genuine fpirit that reigns in this work. We have been content with fuppreffing (efpecially in the firft letters) a great number of *Oriental* * terms and comparifons, which efcaped *Zilia*, though fhe knew the *French* tongue perfectly well when fhe tranflated them : we have only left fo many of them as may fhew the neceffity of retrenching the reft.

We thought it poffible alfo to give a more intelligible turn to certain metaphyfical ftrokes, which might have appeared obfcure ; but this we have done without changing the thought itfelf. This is the only part that the editor has had in this fingular work.

---

* The *French* editor here ufes *Oriental* for *lofty* and *fwelling*, though the *Peruvians*, with refpect to us, are certainly an *Occidental* people.

TO what the editor hath already faid, the tranflator begs leave juft to add, that, as he went trough his tafk with peculiar pleafure, he hopes he has done juftice to a work which appears to him to have great beauty in the original. The *Peruvian* character, as far as we know it from hiftory, joined to that of good fenfe, inflexible virtue, tender fentiments, and unchangeable affections, cannot be more ftrongly and naturally painted than in the letters of *Zilia* ; nor do we often fee the progrefs of the human mind fo correctly and expreffively drawn as in thefe letters.

To this edition are now firft added the letters of *Aza*; the advertifement prefixed to them by the *French* editor fhows by what means they were obtained. We fhall only add here, that by thefe letters the hiftory of *Aza* and *Zilia* is rendered complete.

We prefume, moreover, that in the force and turns of paffion, in delicacy of fentiment, in the variety of incidents, in pertinent reflections, and in dignity, propriety, and elegance of expreffion, they will be found nothing inferior to the moft admired among the letters of *Zilia*.

A N

A N

HISTORICAL INTRODUCTION

TO THE

PERUVIAN LETTERS.

THERE is no people the knowledge of whoſe origin and antiquities is more confined than that of the Peruvians. Scarce do their annals contain the hiſtory of four centuries.

Mancocapac, according to the tradition of theſe people, was their legiſlator and their firſt Inca. The ſun, whom they call their father, and regard as a God, touched they ſay, with that barbarity in which they had for a long time lived, ſent them from heaven two of his children, a ſon and a daughter, who were to give them laws, and to induce them, by cultivating the earth and raiſing of cities, to become rational beings.

It was therefore to *Mancocapac*, and to his wife *Coya Mama Oello Huaco*, that the Peruvians owed thoſe principles, thoſe manners and arts, by which they were made a happy people: before avarice, iſſuing from a world of whoſe exiſtence they had no idea, brought tyrants to their land, whoſe barbarity was a diſgrace to human nature, and the peculiar infamy of the age in which they lived.

The

The particular fituation of the Peruvians at the time the Spaniards made their decent, was the moft favourable to the latter that can be conceived. There had been for fome time paft a report of an oracle which had declared, " That after a certain number of kings reigns, their fhould arrive in that country a wonderful fort of men, fuch as had never yet been feen, who fhould ufurp their government, and deftroy their religion."

Though aftronomy was one of the chief fciences among the Peruvians, they were yet as much fright-ed by prodigies as other nations. Three circles that were feen round the moon; but efpecially certain comets which then appeared; an eagle purfued by other birds; the fea that overflowed its bounds; all made the prediétions of the oracle to appear as infallible as they were fatal.

The eldeft fon of the feventh Inca, whofe name*, in the Peruvian language, declared the fatality of his fpeech, had formerly feen a figure quite different from that of the Peruvians. A robe covered the fpeétre quite to the feet; he had a long beard, and was feated on an unknown animal, which he governed. All this aftonifhed the young prince, to whom the phantom declared that he was defcended from the fun, was the brother of Mancocapac, and that he was called Viracocha.

This ridiculous ftory had been unluckily preferv-ed among the Peruvians, and when they faw the Spaniards with long beards, their limbs covered, and mounted on animals they had never before feen, they took them to be the children of Viracocha, who called himfelf the offspring of the fun; and from thence it came, that the ufurper affumed, by
the

* *Yahuarhuocac*, which literally fignifies, *Bloody tears.*

the ambaſſadors he ſent among them, the title of the deſcendant from the God they adored.

All things bowed before the conquerers. Mankind are every where the ſame. The Spaniards were almoſt generally acknowledged as a kind of gods, whoſe wrath was not to be appeaſed by the moſt profuſe offerings, nor the moſt abject humiliations.

The Peruvians perceiving that the horſes of the Spaniards champed their bits, imagined that thoſe tractable monſters, who partook of their reſpect, and perhaps their worſhip, were nouriſhed by that metal. They therefore daily brought a vaſt quantity of gold and ſilver and laid it before them, by way of offering. We mention this circumſtance merely to ſhew the credulity of the Peruvians, and the facility with which the Spaniards were enabled to ſubdue them.

Whatever homage the Peruvians might render the tyrants, they had diſplayed too much of their riches ever to have any ſort of indulgence from them. A whole people, ſubmiſſive and ſupplicating mercy, were put to the ſword. By the violation of every law of humanity, the Spaniards became abſolute maſters of all the treaſures of one of the richeſt dominions of the earth. *Deſpicable victories!* exclaimed Montagne, on recollecting the vile object of theſe conqueſts. *Never did ambition*, adds he, *never did public animoſities urge mankind to perſecute each other with ſuch horrible hoſtilities, or ſuch deplorable calamities.*

Thus did the Peruvians become the woeful victims of an avaricious people, who at firſt gave no ſigns but thoſe of peace and even friendſhip. An ignorance of our vices, and the ſimplicity of their own manners, threw them into the arms of a baſe enemy. In vain had immenſe tracts of lands and water ſeparated the cities of the ſun from our world, for

for they became our prey, and even the moſt precious part of our dominions.

What a ſight to the Spaniards were the gardens
of the temple of the ſun! where the trees, fruits and
flowers were of ſolid gold, and worked with an art
unknown to Europeans.   The walls of the temple
itſelf lined with the ſame metal: an infinite number
of ſtatues covered with precious ſtones, and an immenſe quantity of other treaſures, till then unknown, dazzled the conquerors of that unhappy people, and made them forget, in the midſt of their
cruelties, that the Peruvians were men.

An analyſis of the manners of theſe unfortunate
people, equally conciſe with that we have here
given of their calamities, ſhall finiſh that introduction which was thought neceſſary to the ſubſe-
quent letters.

The Peruvians were in general of an ingenuous
and humane diſpoſition; the attachment which
they had to their religion, made them rigid ob-
ſervers of the laws, for they regarded them as the
work of Mancocapac, the ſon of that luminary
which they adored.

Though the ſun was the only god to whom they
erected temples, yet they acknowledged, as ſu-
perior to him, a God the Creator, whom they called Pachacamac; and this was with them the ſu-
preme appellation, was rarely pronounced, and
always accompanied with ſigns of the moſt awful
admiration.   They had moreover a great veneration for the moon, which they regarded as the wife
and ſiſter of the ſun.   They conſidered her alſo as
the mother of all things; but they believed, as
do all the Indians, that ſhe would, cauſe the diſſo-
lution of the world, by falling upon the earth, and
thereby deſtroying it.   The thunder, which they
called Yalpor, and the lightning, paſſed among
them

them as minifters of juftice to the fun; and this idea
contributed not a little to infpire them with that
awful refpeĉt they had for the firft Spaniards, whofe
fire arms they took to be the inftruments of thunder.

The opinion of the immortality of the foul was
eftablifhed amoung the Peruvians. They fuppofed,
as do the greateft part of the Indians, that the foul
went into fome unknown regions, where it was
rewarded or punifhed according to its merit.

Gold, and all that was the moft precious among
them, compofed the offerings which they made to
the fun. The *Raymi* was the principal feaft of that
god, to whom they prefented a cup of *mays*, a kind
of ftrong liquor, which they were fkilful in extraĉt-
ing from one of their plants, and of which they
drank even to intoxication after their facrifices.

To the Temple of the Sun there were a hundred doors. The reigning Inca, whom they called
Capa Inca, had the fole right of opening thefe
doors: and alfo to him alone belonged the right of
penetrating into the interior parts of the temple.

The virgins, who were devoted to the Sun, were
there educated, almoft from their birth; and they
there preferved a perpetual virginity, under the
conduĉt of their mamas, or governors; unlefs when
the law had ordained any one of them to efpoufe
the Inca, who was always to marry his fifter, or
when he had no fifter, the firft princefs of the
blood, who was a virgin of the Sun. One of the
principal occupations of thefe virgins was to
prepare diadems for the Incas, of which a fort of
fringe compofed the only ornament.

This temple was decorated with the different
idols of nations who had fubmitted to the Incas,
after they had been made to embrace the worfhip
of

of the fun. The richnefs of the metals, and of the precious ftones with which it was embellifhed, gave it a magnificence and fplendor worthy of that divinity to whom it was confecrated.

The obedience and reverence of the Peruvians for their king, was founded on the belief that the Sun was the father of their monarchs; but their fidelity and affection for them was the fruit of the virtue and equitable government of the Incas themfelves.

The youths of the country were educated with all that care which the happy fimplicity of their morals infpired. Subordination was there fubmitted to with alacrity, becaufe they were early accuftomed to it, and tyranny and pride had there no place. Modefty and mutual affection were the firft principles of their education. Careful to correct each error in its infancy, they who had the charge of their youth, either fuppreffed a rifing paffion, or turned it to the advantage of fociety. There are fome virtues which neceffarily include many others. To give an idea of thofe of the Peruvians, it is fufficient to fay, that before the defcent of the Spaniards, it paffes for an indifputable fact, that no Peruvian was ever known to utter a falfity.

The *Amutas,* or philofophers of that nation, taught their youths the difcoveries they had made in the fciences. The Peruvians were yet in the infancy of that fort of knowledge: they were however in the full vigour of happinefs.

This people had lefs information, lefs knowledge, fewer arts than we have, and yet they had fufficient to provide them with every neceffary of life. The quapas or quipos ✻ ferved them inftead of

our

* The quipos of Peru were alfo in ufe with many other nations of South America.

our writing. Strings of cotton or of guts, with which other strings of different colours were united, reminded them, by means of knots placed at certain distances, of things they desired to remember. By the help of these they preserved their annals, their codes, their rituals, &c. They had also public officers whom they called *Quipocamaios*, to the care of whom their quipos were committed. The finances, the disburfements, the tributes, all matters, all combinations, were as eafily regulated by quipos, as they could have been by writing.

The fage legiflator of Peru, Mancocapac, had inftituted the culture of the earth as a facred right; they enjoyed their lands in common, and the days of their labour were the days of feftivity. Canals of a prodigious extent, diftributed every where refrefhment and fertility; and what is fcarce credible, without any inftrument of iron or fteel, but by the mere force of labour, thefe people were able to overthrow rocks, and cut through the higheft mountains, in order to carry their ftupendous aqueducts, or their public roads, through every part of their dominions.

The Peruvians knew as much of geometry as was neceffary to meafure and divide their lands. Phyfick was there unknown as a fcience, though they had fome medical fecrets which were practifed on particular occafions.

Garcilaffo reports, that they had a fort of mufic, and even fome kinds of poetry. Their poets, whom they called *Hafavec*, compofed a fpecies of tragedy and comedy, which the fons of the caciques*, or the curacas † reprefented, during their feftival times, before the incas and the court.

Morality,

* The caciques were a fort of governors of provinces.
† Sovereigns of a fmall territory. Thefe never appeared

Morality, and the knowledge of the laws neceffary to the welfare of fociety, were therefore the
only fciences in which the Peruvians appear to have
been well fkilled. " It muft be allowed (fays an
hiftorian*) that they have made fuch great advances
in the fcience of policy, and have eftablifhed fo folid
an œconomy, that there will be found but few
nations who can boaft of having excelled them in
thefe matters."

C O N-

peared before the incas and the queens, without offering
them a tribute of the curiofities which the province where
they commanded produced.

   * Puffendorff. Introduction to hiftory.

O F

VOLUME the FIRST.

Letter

C O N-

O F

VOLUME the SECOND.

Letter

LETTERS OF AZA

THE

PERU·VIAN.

Letter

Letter

LETTERS

LETTERS

WRITTEN BY A

PERUVIAN LADY.

LETTER I.

AZA! my dear *Aza!* the cries of thy tender *Zilia*, like a morning vapour, exhale and are diffipated before they arrive in thy prefence: in vain I call thee to my fuccour; in vain I expect thy love to come, and break the chains of my flavery: alas! perhaps the misfortunes I am yet ignorant of are the moft terrible! perhaps thy woes furpafs even mine!

The city of the Sun, delivered to the fury of a barbarous nation, fhould make my eyes overflow with tears; but my grief, my fears, my defpair, are for thee alone.

Dear foul of my life, what wert thou doing in that frightful tumult? Was thy courage fatal or ufelefs to thee? Cruel alternative! diftracting anxiety! O my dear *Aza*, mayeft thou yet live in fafety, and may I fink, if it be needful, under the ills that opprefs me.

B   Since

Since the terrible moment (which fhould have been
fnatched out of the chain of time, and replunged
into the eternal ideas) fince the moment of horror
wherein thefe impious favages bore me away from
the worfhip of the fun, from myfelf, from thy love;
retained in clofe captivity, deprived of all communication, ignorant of the language of thefe fierce
men; I experience only the effects of misfortune,
without being able to difcover the caufe of it. Plunged in an abyfs of obfcurity, my days refemble the
moft dreadful nights.

Far from being affected with my complaints, my
ravifhers are not touch'd even with my tears; equally deaf to my language, and to the cries of my
defpair.

What people are there fo favage as to be unmo-
ved at the figns of anguifh? What dreary defert
could produce human beings infenfible to the voice
of groaning Nature? O the barbarians, favage
mafters of the thunder*, and of the power to ex-
terminate; cruelty is the fole guide of their actions.
Aza! how wilt thou efcape their fury? Where
art thou? in what fituation? If my life is dear to
thee, inform me of thy deftiny.

Alas! how is mine changed. Whence can it be
that days, in themfelves fo like one another, fhould,
with refpect to me, have fuch fatal differences?
Time rolls on, darknefs fucceeds light, nothing in
nature appears out of order? but I, of late fupreme-
ly happy, lo I am fallen into the horror of defpair!
nor was there an interval to prepare me for this fearful change.

'Thou knoweft, O delight of my heart, that on that
terrible day, that day for ever dreadful, the triumph
of our union was to have fhone forth. Scarce did

it

* Alluding to the cannon.

it begin to appear, when impatient to execute a project which my tendernefs had infpired me with in
the night, I ran to my *Quipos* ＊, and, taking advantage of the filence which then reigned in the temple, haftened to knot them, in hopes that by their
affiftance I might render immortal the hiftory of our
love and our felicity.

As I proceeded in my work, the undertaking appeared to me lefs difficult: the clue of innumerable
threads by degrees grew under my fingers a faithful
painting of our actions and our fentiments; as it was
heretofore the interpreter of our thoughts during
the long intervals of our abfence from each other.
Wholly taken up with my employment, I forgot
how time paffed when a confufed noife awakened
my fpirits and put my heart in a flutter. I thought
the happy moment was arrived, and that the hundred gates‡ were opening to give a free paffage to
the fun of my days: precipitately I hid my *Quipos*
under a lappet of my robe, and ran to meet thee.

But how horrible was the fpectacle that appeared
before my eyes! The fearful idea of it will never be
effaced out of my memory.

The pavement of the temple ftained with blood；
the image of the fun trodden under foot；our affright-
ed virgins flying before a troop of furious foldiers,
who maffacred all that oppofed their paffage; our
Mamas✝ expiring under their wounds, their garments ftill burning with the fire of the thunder ; the

B 2   groans

＊ A great number of ftrings of different colours, which
the *Indians* ufe for want of writing, in accounting the pay
of their troops, and the number of their people. Some
authors pretend, that they make ufe of them alfo to tranfmit to pofterity the memorable actions of their *Incas*.

‡ In the temple of the Sun were a hundred gates, which
the *Inca* only had power to have opened.

✝ A kind of Governantes over the virgins of the Sun.

groans of difmay, the cries of rage, fpreading dread and horror on every fide, brought me at laft to a fenfe of my mifery.

Being returned to myfelf, I found that by a natural, and almoft involuntary motion, I was got behind the altar, which I embraced. There I faw the barbarians pafs by : I did not dare to give free paffage to my panting breath, for fear it fhould coft me my life. I remarked, however, that the effects of their cruelty abated at the fight of the precious ornaments that overfpread the temple; that they feized thofe whofe luftre ftruck them moft fenfibly; and that they even plucked off the plates of gold that lined the walls. I judged that theft was the motive of their barbarity, and that, to avoid death, my only way was to conceal myfelf from their fight. I defigned to have got out of the temple, to have been conducted to thy palace, to have demanded fuccour of the *Capa Inca**, and an afylum for my companions and me : but no fooner did I attempt to ftir, than I was arrefted. Oh my dear *Aza!* then did I tremble! thefe impious men dared to lay their hands upon the daughter of the fun.

Torn from the facred abode, dragged ignominioufly out of the temple, I faw for the firft time the threfhold of the celeftial gate, which I ought not to have paffed but with the enfigns of royalty‡. Inftead of the flowers which fhould have been ftrewed under my feet, I faw the ways covered with blood and carnage : inftead of the honours of the throne, which I was to have partaken of with thee; I find myfelf a flave under the laws of tyranny,

* The general name of the reigning *Incas.*

‡ The virgins confecrated to the Sun entered the temple almoft as foon as born, and never came out till the day of their marriage.

ranny, fhut up in an obfcure prifon, the place that I occupy in the univerfe is bounded by the extent of my being. A mat, bathed with tears, receives my body fatigued by the torments of my foul : But dear fupport of my life, how light will all thefe evils be to me, if I can but learn that thou yet breatheft.

In the midft of this horrible defolation, I know not by what happy chance I have preferved my *Quipos*. I have them in poffeffion, my dear *Aza* ; they are the treafure of my heart, as they ferve to interpret both thy love and mine : the fame knots which fhall inform thee of my exiftence, changing their form under thy hands, will inftruct me alfo in my deftiny. Alas ! by what way fhall I convey them to thee ? By what addrefs can they be reftored to me again ? I am ignorant at prefent : but the fame underftanding which taught us their ufe, will fuggeft to us the means to deceive our tyrants. Whoever the faithful *Chaqui* * may be that fhall bring thee this precious depofite, I fhall envy his happinefs. He will fee thee, my dear *Aza* ; and I would give all the days allotted me by the fun to enjoy thy prefence one moment.

LETTER II.

MAY the tree of virtue, my dear *Aza*, for ever fpread its fhadow over the pious citizen who received under my window the myfterious tiffue of my thoughts, and delivered it into thy hands. May *Paca-Camac* † prolong his years, as the recompence of his addrefs in conveying to me divine pleafures with thy anfwer.

The treafures of love are open to me ; I draw from thence a delicious joy that inebriates my foul.

B 3 While

* Meffenger.
† The Creator God, more powerful than the Sun.

While I unravel the secrets of thy heart, my own bathes itself in a sea of perfumes. Thou livest, and the chains that were to unite us are not broken. So much felicity was the object of my desires, but not of my hopes.

Whilst I abandoned all thought of myself, my fears for thee deprived me of all pleasure. Thou restorest to me all that I had lost. I taste deep draughts of the sweet satisfaction of pleasing thee, of being praised by thee, of being approved by him I love. But, dear *Aza*, while I swim in these delights, I do not forget that I owe to thee what I am. As the rose draws his brilliant colours from the rays of the sun, so the charms which please thee in my spirit and sentiments are the benefits of thy luminous genius; nothing is mine, but my tenderness.

If thou hadst been an ordinary man, I had remained in that ignorance to which my sex is condemned; but thou, not the slave of custom, hast broken the barrier, in order to elevate me to thyself. Thou didst not suffer a being like thy own, to be confined to the humble advantage of only giving life to thy posterity: it was thy pleasure that our *Amulas* * should adorn my understanding with their sublime intelligences. But O light of my life, could I have resolved to abandon my tranquil ignorance, and engage in the painful occupation of study, had it not been for the desire of pleasing thee? Without a desire to merit thy esteem, thy confidence, thy respect, by virtues which fortify love, and which love renders voluptuous, I had been only the object of thy eyes; absence would already have effaced me out of thy remembrance.

But,

* *Indian* Philosophers.

But, alas! if thou loveſt me ſtill, why am I in ſlavery? Caſting a look upon the walls of my pri-ſon, my joy diſappears, horror ſeizes me, and my fears are renewed. They have not robbed thee of liberty, yet thou comeſt not to my ſuccour: Thou haſt been informed of my ſituation, and it is not changed. No, my dear *Aza*, among thoſe ſavage people, whom thou calleſt *Spaniards*, thou art not ſo free as thou imagineſt thyſelf. I behold as many ſigns of ſlavery in the honours which they render thee, as in my own captivity.

Thy goodneſs ſeduces thee; thou thinkeſt the promiſes, which thoſe barbarians make thee by their interpreters, ſincere, becauſe thy own words are inviolable; but I, who underſtand not their language, whom they think not worthy to be de-ceived, behold their actions.

Thy ſubjects take them for gods, and join their party. O my dear *Aza*, wretched the people who are determined by fear! Extricate thyſelf from thy error, and ſuſpect the falſe goodneſs of theſe foreigners. Abandon thy empire, ſince the *Incha Viracocha* * has predicted its deſtruction.

Redeem thy life and thy liberty at the price of thy power, thy grandeur, and thy treaſures; the gifts of nature alone will then remain to thee, and our days ſhall paſs in ſafety.

Rich in the poſſeſſion of our hearts, great by our virtues, powerful by our moderation, we ſhall in a cottage enjoy the heaven, the earth, and our mutual tenderneſs.

Thou wilt be more a king in a reigning over my ſoul, than in doubting of the affection of a people

B 4 without

* *Viracocha* was looked upon as a God, and the *Indians* firmly believe that at his death he predicted that the *Spa-niards* ſhould dethrone one of his deſcendants.

without number : my fubmiffion to thy will fhall
caufe thee to enjoy, without tyranny, the undif-
puted right of commanding. While I obey thee,
I will make thy empire refound with my joyous
fongs ; thy diadem * fhall be always the work of
my hands, and thou fhalt lofe nothing of royalty
but the cares and fatigues.

How often, dear foul of my life, has thou com-
plained of the duties of thy rank ? How have the
ceremonies, which accompanied thy vifits, made
thee envy the lot of thy fubjeĉts ? Thy wifh was
to live for me only. Art thou now afraid to lofe
fo many conftraints ? Shall I be no more that *Zilia*,
whom thou preferredft to thy empire ? I cannot
entertain the thought : my heart is not changed,
and why fhould there be a change in thine ?

I love ; the fame *Aza* who reigned in my heart
the firft moment I faw him, is for ever before me :
continually do my thoughts recall that happy day,
when thy father, my fovereign lord, gave thee
for the firft time a fhare of that power, referved
for him only, of entering the inner part of the
temple ‡. Fancy ftill figures to me the agreeable
fpeĉtacle of our virgins, who, being there affembled, received a new luftre from the admirable order that reigns among them : fo in a garden we fee
the arrangement of the fineft flowers add a brillian-
cy to their beauty.

Thou appearedft in the midft of us like a rifing
fun, whofe tender light prepares the ferenity of a
fine day : the fire of thy eyes overfpread our cheeks
with the blufhes of modefty, and our looks were
held captive in fweet confufion : thy eyes, at the
fame

* The diadem of the *Incas* was a kind of fringe wrought
by the virgins of the Sun.
‡ The reigning *Inca* alone has a right to enter into the
temple of the Sun.

fame time, fhot forth a brilliant joy; for never
before had they met fo many beauties together.
The *Capa-Inca* was the only man we had till then
feen. Aftonifhment and filence reigned on every fide.
I know not what were the thoughts of my companions: but the fentiments that attacked my own
heart, who can exprefs? For the firft time I had
the united fenfe of trouble, inquietude, and pleafure. Confufed with the agitations of my foul, I
was going to hide myfelf from thy fight: but thou
turnedft thy fteps towards me, and I was retained
by refpect. O my dear *Aza*, the remembrance of
this firft moment of my happinefs will be always
dear to me. The found of thy voice, like the
melodious chanting of our hymns, conveyed into
my veins that foft tremor, and holy refpect, which
is infpired by the prefence of the divinity.

Trembling, difmay'd, my timidity had taken
from me even the ufe of my fpeech: but, embol-
den'd at laft by the foftnefs of thy words, I dared
to lift up my looks towards thee, and meet thine.
No, death itfelf fhall never efface from my memory
the tender movements of our fouls at this meeting,
and how in an inftant they were blended together.

If we could doubt of our original, my dear *Aza*,
this glance of light would have deftroyed our un-
certainty. What other principle, but that of fire,
could have tranfmitted betwixt us this lively intelligence of hearts, which was communicated,
fpread, and felt with an inexplicable rapidity?

I was too ignorant of the effects of love, not to
be deceived by it. With an imagination full of the
fublime theology of our *Cucipatas* *, I took the fire
which animated me for a divine agitation; I
thought the Sun had manifefted to me his will by

B 5 thee

* Priefts of the Sun.

thee his organ, that he chofe me for his felected
fpoufe! I fighed in rapture!—but after thy departure, examining my heart, I found there nothing but thy image.

What a change, my dear *Aza*, did thy prefence
make in me! All objects appeared to me new, and
it feemed as if I now faw my fellow virgins the
firft time. How did their beauty brighten! I could
not bear their prefence, but, retiring afide, gave
way to the anxiety of my foul, when one of them
came to waken me out of my reverie, by giving
me frefh matter to heighten it: fhe informed me,
that, being thy neareft relation, I was deftined to
be thy wife, as foon as my age would permit that
union.

I was ignorant of the laws of thy empire *;
but, after I had feen thee, my heart was too much
enlightened not to have the idea of happinefs in
an union with thee. Far, however, from knowing the whole extent of this union, and accuftomed to the facred name of Spoufe of the Sun, my
hopes were bounded to the feeing of thee daily,
the adoring of thee, and offering my vows to thee,
as to that divinity.

Thou, my amiable *Aza*, thou thyfelf filledft up
the meafure of my delight, by informing me that
the auguft rank of thy wife would affociate me to
thy heart, to thy throne, to thy glory, to thy virtues; that I fhould inceffantly enjoy thofe fo precious converfations, thofe converfations fo fhort in
proportion to our defires, which would adorn my
mind with the perfections of thy foul, and add to
my felicity the delicious hope of being hereafter a
happinefs to thee.

O my

* The laws of the *Indians* obliged the *Incas* to marry their
fifters; and when they had none, to take the firft princefs
of the blood of the *Incas* that was a virgin of the Sun.

O my dear *Aza*, how flattering to my heart was
that impatience of thine, fo often exprefled on account of my youth, which retarded our union!
How long did the courfe of two years appear to
thee, and yet how fhort was their duration! Alas!
the fortunate moment was arrived! What fatality
rendered it fo woeful? What God was it who punifhed innocence and virtue in this manner? or,
what infernal power feparated us from ourfelves?
Horror feizes me,—my heart is rent,—my tears
bedew my work. *Aza! my dear Aza!*

LETTER III.

IT is thou, dear light of my foul, it is thou who
calleft me back to life. Would I preferve it, if
I was not fure that death, by a fingle ftroke, would
mow down thy days and mine? I touched the moment in which the fpark of divine fire, wherewith
the fun animates our being, was going to expire.
Laborious nature was already preparing to give
another form to that portion of matter which belonged to her in me: I was dying; thou waft
lofing for ever half of thyfelf, when my love reftored my life, which I now facrifice to thee. But
how can I inform thee of the furprifing things that
have happened to me? How fhall I call back ideas
that were confufed even when I received them, and
which the time that is fince paffed renders ftill lefs
intelligible?

Scarcely, my dear *Aza*, had I entrufted our faithful *Chaqui* with the laft tiffue of my thoughts,
when I heard a great motion in our habitation:
about midnight two of my ravifhers came to hurry
me out of my gloomy retreat, with as much violence as they had employed in fnatching me from
the temple of the Sun.

Though

Though the night was very dark, they made me travel fo far, that, finking under the fatigue, they were obliged to carry me into a houfe, which I could perceive, notwithftanding the obfcurity, it was exceeding difficult to get into.

I was truft into a place more ftrait and inconvenient than my prifon had been. Ah, my dear *Aza!* could I perfuade thee of what I do not comprehend myfelf, if thou wert not affured that a lie never fullied the lips of a child of the Sun * ?

This houfe, which I judged to be very great by the quantity of people it contained, was not fixed to the ground, but being as it were fufpended, kept in a continual balancing motion.

O light of my mind, *Ticaiviracocha* fhould have filled my foul like thine with his divine fcience, to have enabled me to comprehend this prodigy. All that I know of it is, that this dwelling was not built by a being friendly to mankind : for fome moments after I had entered it, the continual motion of it, joined to a noxious fmell, made me fo violently ill, that I am furprized I did not die of the malady. This was the beginning only of my pains.

A pretty long time paffed, and I had no confiderable fuffering, when one morning I was frighted out of fleep by a noife more hideous than that of *Yalpa*. Our habitation received fuch fhocks as the earth will experience, when the moon by her fall fhall reduce the univerfe to duft ‡. The cries of human voices, joined to this wild uproar, rendered it ftill more frightful. My fenfes, feized with a fecret horror, conveyed to my foul nothing but the idea of deftruction, not of myfelf only, but of all nature. I thought the peril univerfal; I trembled for

* It paffes for certain that no *Peruvian* ever lied.
‡ The *Indians* believe that the end of the world will be brought about by the fall of the moon upon the earth.

for thy life : my dread grew at laſt to the utmoſt
excefs, when I faw a company of men in fury, with
bloody countenances and cloaths, ruſh tumultuouſ-
ly into my chamber. I could not ſupport the terrible ſpeƈacle ; my ſtrength and underſtanding left
me : ſtill am I ignorant of the confequence of this
terrible event. But when I recovered, I found
myſelf in a pretty handſome bed, ſurrounded by
feveral favages, who were not however, any of
the cruel *Spaniards.*

Canſt thou imagine to thyſelf my ſurprize, when
I found myſelf in a new dwelling, among new
men, without being able to comprehend how this
change could be brought about ? I ſhut my eyes,
the better to recolleƈ myſelf, and be aſſured whether I was alive, or whether my foul had not quitted my body to pafs into unknown regions *.

I confefs to thee, dear idol of my heart, that,
fatigued with an odious life, diſheartened at ſuffering torments of every kind, preſſed down under
the weight of my horrible deſtiny, I regarded with
indifference the end of my being which I felt ap-
proaching : I conſtantly refuſed all the ſuſtenance
that was offered me, and in a few days was on the
verge of the fatal term, which I beheld without
regret.

The decay of my ſtrength annihilated my ſentiments : already my enfeebled imagination received no images but like thofe of a ſlight defign traced
by a trembling hand ; already the objeƈs which
had moſt affeƈted me, excited in me only that
vague fenfation which we feel when we indulge to
an indeterminate reverie : almoſt I was no more.
This ſtate, my dear *Aza,* is not fo uxprefs the: is
:nhot even-ht.

* The *Indians* believe that the foul, after death, goes
into unknown places, to be there recompenfed or puniſhed
according to its deferts.

thought. At a diftance it frightens us, becaufe
we think of it with all our powers : when it is arrived, enfeebled by the gradations of pain which conduct us to it, the decifive moment appears only as
the moment of repofe. A natural propenfity which
carries us towards futurity, even that futurity
which will never exift for us, reanimated my fpirit,
and tranfported it into thy palace. I thought I arrived there at the inftant when thou hadft received the news of my death. I reprefented to myfelf thy pale disfigured image, fuch as lily appears
when fcorched by the burning heat of noon. Is
the moft tender love then fometimes barbarous? I
rejoiced at thy grief, and excited it by forrowful
adieus. I found a fweetnefs, perhaps a pleafure,
in diffufing the poifon of regret over thy days;
and the fame love which rendered me cruel, tore
my heart by the horror of thy pains. At laft, a-
waken'd as from a profound fleep, penetrated with
thy agony, trembling for thy life, I called for help,
and again beheld the light.

Shall I fee thee again, thou, the dear arbiter of
my exiftence? Alas ! who can affure me of it.
I know not where I am : perhaps it is far diftant
from thee ! But fhould we be feparated by the immenfe fpaces inhabited by the children of the Sun,
the light cloud of my thoughts fhall hover inceffantly about thee.

LETTER IV.

WHATEVER the love of life be, my dear
Aza, pains diminifh, defpair extinguifhes
it. idea of de tempt in which nature feems to hold
our nature. I abandoning it to defpair, fhocks us
at firft : afterward, the impoffibility of working

our

our deliverance proves such an humbling circumstance, that it leads us to a disgust of ourselves.

I live no longer in, nor for myself: every instant in which I breathe, is a sacrifice which I make to thy love, and from day to day it becomes more painful. If time bring some solace to the ills that consume me, far from clearing up my present condition, it seems to render it more obscure. All that surrounds me is unknown, all is new, all engages my curiosity, and nothing can satisfy it. In vain I employ my attention and efforts to understand or be understood ; both are equally impossible to me. Wearied with so many fruitless pains, I thought to dry up the source of them, by depriving my eyes of the impressions they receive from objects. I persisted for some time in keeping them shut : but the voluntary darkness, to which I condemned myself, served only to relieve my modesty : offended continually at the presence of these men, whose officious kindnesses are so many torments, my soul was not the less agitated : shut up in myself, my inquietudes were not the less sharp, and the desire to express them was the more violent. On the other hand, the impossibility of making myself understood, spread an anguish over my organs, which is not less insupportable than the pains which a more apparent reality would cause. How cruel is this situation !

Alas! I thought I had begun to understand some words of the savage Spaniards : I found some agreement with our august language : I flattered myself that in a short time I should come to explain myself with them. Far from finding the same advantage among my new tyrants, they express themselves with so much rapidity that I cannot even distinguish the inflexions of their voice. All circumstances make me judge that they are not of the same
nation :

nation : and by the difference of their manners and apparent character, one eafily divines that Pacha-camac has diftributed to them in great difproportion the elements of which he formed human kind. The grave and fierce air of the firft fhews that they are compofed of the fame matter as the hardeft metals. Thefe feem to have fliped out of the hands of the creator the moment he had collected together only air and fire for their formation. The fcornful eyes, the gloomy and tranquil mien of the former, fhew-ed fufficiently that they were cruel in cold blood ; which the inhumanity of their actions has too well proved. The fmiling countenance of the latter, the fweetnefs of their looks, a certain hafte in all their actions, which feems to be a hafte of good will, prevents me in their favour, but I remark contradictions in their conduct which fufpends my judgment.

Two of thefe favages feldom quit the fides of my bed : one, which I guefs to be the *Cacique* * by his air of grandeur, feems to fhew me, in his way, a great deal of refpect : the other gives me part of the affiftance which my malady requires ; but his goodnefs is fevere, his fuccours are cruel, and his familiarity imperious.

The moment when, recovered from my fit, I found myfelf in their power, this latter (for I have obferved him well) more bold than the reft, would take me by the hand, which I drew away with in-expreffible confufion. He feemed to be furprized at my refiftance, and without any regard to my modefty, took hold of it again immediately. Feeble, dying, and fpeaking only fuch words as were not underftood, could I hinder him ? He held it, my dear *Aza*, as long as he thought proper ; and

* Cacique is a kind of governor of a province.

and since that time, I am obliged to give it him myself several times every day, in order to avoid such disputes as always turn to my disadvantage.

This kind of ceremony * seems to me a superstition of these people ; they imagine they find something there which indicates the nature of a distemper ; but it must doubtless be their own nation that feel the effects of it : for I perceive none ; I suffer continually by an inward fire that consumes me, and have scarce strength enough left to knot my *Quipos*. In this occupation I employ as much time as my weakness will permit me : the knots, which strike my senses, seem to give more reality to my thoughts : the kind of resemblance which I imagine they have with words, causes an illusion which deceives my pain : I think I speak to thee, tell thee of my love, assure thee of my vows and my tenderness : the sweet error is my support, and my life. If the excess of my burthen obliges me to interrupt my work, I groan at thy absence. Given up thus intirely to my tenderness, there is not one of my moments which belongs not to thee.

Alas ! what other use can I make of them ? O my dear *Aza!* if thou wert not the master of my soul ; if the chains of love did not bind me inseparably to thee ; plunged in an abyss of obscurity, could I turn my thoughts away from the light of my life ? Thou art the sun of my days ; thou enlightenest them ; thou prolongest them, and they are thine. Thou cherishest me, and I suffer myself to live. What wilt thou do for me ? Thou lovest me, and I have my reward.

LET-

---

* The *Indians* have no knowledge of physick.

LETTER V.

WHAT have I fuffered, my dear *Aza*, fince I confecrated to thee my laft knots! The lofs of my *Quipos* was yet wanting to complete my pains: but when my officious perfecutors perceived that work to augment my diforder, they deprived me of the ufe of them.

At laft they have reftored to me the treafure of my tendernefs; but with many tears did I purchafe it. Only this expreffion of my fentiments had I remaining, the mere forrowful confolation of painting my grief to thee: and could I lofe it, and not defpair?

My ftrange deftiny has fnatched from me even the relief which the unhappy find in fpeaking of their pains. One is apt to think there is pity when one is heard, and from the participation of forrow arifes fome comfort: I cannot make myfelf underftood, and am furrounded with gaiety.

I cannot even enjoy that new kind of entertainment to which the inability of communicating my thoughts reduces me. Environed with importunate perfons, whofe attentive looks difturb the compofed folicitude of my foul, I forget the faireft prefent which nature has made us, the power to render our ideas impenetrable without the concurrence of our will. I am fometimes afraid that thefe curious favages difcover the difadvantageous reflections with which I am infpired by the oddnefs of their conduct.

One moment deftroys the opinion which another had given me of their character: for if I am fwayed by the frequent oppofition of their wills to mine, I cannot doubt but they believe me their flave, and that their power is tyrannical.

Not

Not to reckon up an infinite number of other contradictions, they refuse me, my dear *Aza*, even the necessary aliments for the sustenance of life, and the liberty of chusing what place I would lie in : they keep me, by a kind of violence, in the bed, which is become insupportable to me.

On the other side, if I reflect on the extreme concern they have shewn for the preservation of my days, and the respect with which the services they render me are accompanied, I am tempted to believe that they take me for a species superior to human kind.

Not one of them appears before me without bending his body, more or less, as we used to do in worshipping the Sun. The *Cacique* seems to attempt to imitate the ceremonial of the *Incas* on the days of *Raymi* * : he kneels down very nigh my bed side, and continues a considerable time in that painful posture : sometimes he keeps silent, and, with his eyes cast down, seems to think profoundly : I see in his countenance that respectful confusion which the great name ‡ inspires us with when spoken aloud. If he finds an opportunity of taking hold of my hand, he puts his mouth to it with the same veneration that we have for the sacred diadem †. Sometimes he utters a great number of words, which are not at all like the ordinary language of his nation : the found of them is more soft, more distinct, and more harmonious. He joins to this that air of concern which is the forerunner of tears, those sighs which express the
necessities

---

* The *Raymi* was the principal feast of the Sun, when the *Incas* and priests adored him on their knees.

‡ The great name was *Pachacamac*, which they spoke but seldom, and always with great signs of adoration.

† They kissed the diadem of *Mancocapac* in the same manner as the Roman Catholicks kiss the relicks of their saints.

neceffities of the foul, the moft plaintive action, and all that ufually accompanies the defire of obtaining favours! Alas! my dear *Aza*, if he knew me well, if he was not in fome error with regard to my being, what prayer could he have to addrefs to me?

Muft they not be an idolatrous nation? I have not yet feen any adoration paid by them to the Sun : perhaps they make women the object of their worfhip. Before the great *Manco-cupac* * brought down to earth the will of the Sun, our anceftors deified whatever ftruck them with dread or pleafure : perhaps thefe favages feel thefe two fentiments with regard to women.

But if they adore me, would they add to my misfortunes the hideous conftraint in which they keep me? No; they would endeavour to pleafe me; they would obey the tokens of my will : I fhould be free, and releafed from this odious habitation : I fhould go in fearch of the mafter of my foul, one of whofe looks would efface the memory of all thefe misfortunes.

LETTER VI.

WHAT an horrible furprize, my dear *Aza!* how are our woes augmented! how deplorable is our condition! our evils are without remedy : I have only to tell thee of them and to die.

At laft they have permitted me to get up, and with hafte I availed myfelf of the liberty. I drew myfelf to a fmall window, which I opened with all the precipitation that my curiofity infpired. What did I fee? Dear love of my life, I fhall not find
                                    expreffions

* The firft Legiflator of the *Indians. See the hiftory of the Incas.*

expreffions to paint the excefs of my aftonifhment, and the incurable defpair that feized me, when I difcovered round me nothing but that terrible element, the very fight of which makes me tremble!

My firft glance did but too well inform me what occafioned the troublefome motion of our dwelling. I am in one of thofe floating houfes which the *Spaniards* made ufe of to arrive at our unhappy countries, and of which a very imperfect defcription had been given me.

Conceive, dear *Aza*, what difmal ideas entered my foul with this fatal knowledge. I am certain that they are carrying me from thee: I breathe no more the fame air, nor do I inhabit the fame element. Thou wilt ever be ignorant where I am, whether I love thee, whether I exift; even the diffolution of my being will not appear an event confiderable enough to be conveyed to thee. Dear arbiter of my days, of what value will my life be to thee hereafter? Permit me to render to the divinity an infupportable benefit, which I can no more enjoy: I fhall not fee thee again, and I will live no longer.

In lofing what I love, the univerfe is annihilated to me: it is now nothing but a vaft defart, which I fill with the cries of my love. Hear them, dear object of my tendernefs; be touched with them, and fuffer me to die!

What error feduces me? My dear *Aza*, it is not thou that makeft me live: it is timid Nature, which fhuddering with horror, lends this voice, more powerful than its own, to retard an end which to her is always formidable:—but it is over; —the moft ready means fhall deliver me from her regrets.————

Let the fea for ever fwallow up in its waves my unhappy tendernefs, my life, and my defpair.—

Receive,

Receive, moſt unfortunate *Aza*, receive the laſt
ſentiments of my heart, which never admitted but
thy image, was willing to live but for thee, and
dies full of thy love. I love thee, I think it, I
feel it ſtill, and I tell it thee for the laſt time——

LETTER VII.

AZA, thou haſt not loſt all : I breathe, and
thou reigneſt ſtill in one heart. The vigi-
lance of thoſe who watch me defeated my fatal deſign, and I have only the ſhame left of having at-
tempted its execution. It would be too long to
inform thee of the circumſtances of an enterprize
that failed as ſoon as it was projeȼted. Should I
have dared ever to lift up my eyes to thee, if thou
had been a witneſs of my paſſion ?

My reaſon, ſubjeȼted to deſpair, was no longer
a ſuccour to me : my life ſeemed to me worth
nothing : I had forgot thy love.

How cruel is a cool temper after fury ! How different are the points of ſight on the ſame objeȼts !
In the horror of deſpair ferocity is taken for courage, and the fear of ſuffering for firmneſs of
mind. Let a look, a ſurprize call us back to ourſelves, and we find that weakneſs only was the
principle of our heroiſm ; that repentance is the
fruit of it, and contempt the recompence.

The knowledge of my fault is the moſt ſevere
puniſhment of it. Abandoned to the bitterneſs of
repentance, buried under the veil of ſhame, I hold
myſelf at a diſtance, and fear that my body occupies too much ſpace : I would hide it from the
light : my tears flow in abundance ; my grief
is calm, not a ſigh expires, though I am quite
given up to it. Can I do too much to expiate my
crime ? It was againſt thee.

In

In vain, for two days together, thefe beneficent
favages have endeavoured to make me a partaker
of the joy that tranfports them. I am in continual
doubt what can be the caufe of this joy ; but, even
if I knew it better, I fhould not think myfelf
worthy to fhare in their feftivals. Their dances,
their jovial exclamations, a red liquor like *Mays* *,
of which they drink abundantly, their eagernefs to
view the fun wherever they can perceive him,
would fully convince me that their rejoicings were
in honour of that divine luminary, if the con-
duft of the *Cacique* was conformable to that of the
reft.

But, far from taking part in the publick joy,
fince the fault I committed, he interefts himfelf
only in my forrow. His zeal is more refpeftful,
his cares are more affiduous, and his attention is
more exaft and curious.

He underftood that the continual prefence of the
favages of his train about me, was an addition to
my afflidion ; he has delivered me from their troublefome officioufnefs, and I have now fcarcely any
but his to fupport.

Wouldft thou believe it, my dear *Aza*, there are
fome moments in which I feel a kind of fweetnefs
in thefe mute dialogues ; the fire of his eyes recalls
to my mind the image of that which I have feen in
thine : the fimilitude is fuch that it feduces my
heart. Alas that this illufion is tranfient, and that
the regrets which follow it are durable ! they will
end only with my life, fince I live for thee alone.

LET-

* *Mays* is a plant whereof the *Indians* make a very
ftrong and falutary drink, which they offer to the Sun
on feftival days, and get drunk with after the facrifice is
over. *See Hiftory of the Incas.* Vol. II.

LETTER VIII.

WHEN a fingle object unites all our thoughts, my dear *Aza*, we intereft ourfelves no far-ther in events than as we find them affimilated to our own cafe. If thou waft not the only mover of my foul, could I have paffed, as I have juft done, from the horror of defpair to the moft flattering hope? The *Cacique* had before feveral times in vain at-tempted to entice me to that window, which I now cannot look at without fhuddering. At laft, pre-vailed on by frefh folicitations, I fuffered myfelf to be conducted to it. Oh, my dear *Aza*, how well was I recompenced for my complaifance!

By an incomprehenfible miracle, in making me look through a kind of hollow cane, he fhewed me the earth at a diftance; whereas, without the help of this wonderful machine, my eyes could not have reached it.

At the fame time, he made me underftand by figns, (which begin to grow familiar to me) that we were going to that land, and that the fight of it was the only caufe of thofe rejoicings which I took for a facrifice to the fun.

I was immediately fenfible of all the benefit of this difcovery : Hope, like a ray of light, glanced directly to the bottom of my heart.

They are certainly carrying me to this land which they have fhewn me, and which is evident-ly a part of thy empire, fince the Sun there fheds his beneficent rays *. I am no longer in the fet-ters of the cruel *Spaniards* : Who then fhall hinder my returning under thy laws ?

Yes,

---

* The *Indians* know not our hemifphere, and believe that the fun enlightens only the land of his children.

Yes, my dear *Aza*, I go to be reunited to what I love: my love, my reaſon, my deſires, all aſſure me of it. I fly into thy arms; a torrent of joy overflows my ſoul; the paſt is vaniſhed; my misfortunes are ended, they are forgotten: Futurity alone employs me, and is my ſole good.

Aza, my dear hope, I have not loſt thee; I ſhall ſee thy countenance, thy robes, thy ſhadow, I ſhall love thee, and tell thee of it with my own mouth: Can any torments efface ſuch a felicity?

LETTER IX.

HOW long are the days, my dear *Aza*, when one computes their paſſage! Time, like ſpace, is known only by its limits. Our hopes ſeem to me the hopes of time; if they quit us, or are not diſtinctly-marked, we perceive no more of their duration than of the air which fills the vaſt expanſe.

Ever ſince the fatal inſtant of our ſeparation, my heart and ſoul, worn with misfortune, continued ſunk in that total abſence, that oblivion which is the horror of nature, the image of nothing: The days paſſed away without my regarding them, for not a hope fixed my attention to their length. But hope now marks every inſtant of them; their duration ſeems to me infinite; and what ſurprizes me moſt of all is, that, in recovering the tranquillity of my ſpirit, I recover at the ſame time a facility of thinking.

Since my imagination has been opened to joy, a crowd of thoughts preſent themſelves, and employ it even to fatigue: Projects of pleaſure and happineſs ſucceed one another alternately; new ideas find an eaſy reception, and ſome are even imprinted without my ſearch, and before I perceive it.

C

Within

Within thefe two days, I underftand feveral
words of the *Cacique*'s language, which I was not
before acquainted with. But they are only terms
applicable to objects, not expreffive of my thoughts,
nor fufficient to make me underftand thofe of
others : They give me fome lights however, which
were neceffary for my fatisfaction.

I know that the name of the *Cacique* is *Deterville*; that of our floating houfe, a *Ship*; and that
of the country we are going to, *France*.

The latter at firft frightened me, as I did not
remember to have heard any province of thy kingdom called fo : But reflecting on the infinite number of countries under thy dominion, the names
of which I have forgot, my fear quickly vanifhed. Could it long fubfift with that folid confidence
which the fight of the Sun gives me inceffantly ?
No, my dear *Aza*, that divine luminary enlightens
only his children. To doubt this would be criminal in me : I am returning into thy empire ; I am
on the point of feeing thee ; I run to my felicity.

Amidft the tranfports of my joy, gratitude prepares me a delicious pleafure. Thou wilt load
with honour and riches the beneficent *Cacique*,
who fhall reftore us one to the other : He fhall
bear into his own country the remembrance of
Zilia; the recompence of his virtue fhall render
him ftill more virtuous, and his happinefs fhall be
thy glory.

Nothing can compare, my dear *Aza*, to the
kindnefs he fhews me. Far from treating me as
his flave, he feems to be mine. He is now alto-
gether as complaifant to me, as he was contradic-
tory during my ficknefs. My perfon, my inquietudes, my amufements, feem to make up his whole
employment, and to engage all his care. I admit
his offices with lefs confufion, fince cuftom and re-
flexion

flexion have informed me that I was in an error with regard to the idolatry I fufpected him guilty of.

Not that he does not continue to repeat much the fame demonftrations which I took for worfhip : but the tone, the air, and manner he makes ufe of, perfuade me that it is only a diverfion in his country manner.

He begins by making me pronounce diftinctly fome words in his language, and he knows well that the Gods do not fpeak. As foon as I have repeated after him, *oui, je vous aime,* [*yes I love you*] or elfe, *je promets d'etre a vous,* [*I promife to be yours*] joy expands over his countenance, he kiffes my hands with tranfport, and with an air of gayety quite contrary to that gravity which accompanies divine adoration.

Eafy as I am on the head of religion, I am not quite fo with regard to the country from whence he comes. His language and his apparel are fo different from ours, that they fometimes fhock my confidence : uneafy reflections fometimes cloud over my dear hope ; I pafs fucceffively from fear to joy, and from joy to inquietude.

Fatigued with the confufion of my thoughts, fick of the uncertainties that torment me, I had refolved to think no more on the fubject : But what can abate the anxiety of a foul deprived of all communication, that acts only on itfelf, and is excited to reflect by fuch important interefts ? I cannot exprefs my impatience, my dear *Aza* ; I fearch for information with an eagernefs that devours me, and yet continually find myfelf in the moft profound obfcurity. I know that the privation of a fenfe may in fome refpects deceive ; and yet I fee with furprize, that the ufe of all mine drag me on from error to error. Would the

C 2

intelli-

intelligence of tongues be a key to the foul? O my dear *Aza*, how many grievous truths do I fee through my misfortunes! But far from me be thefe troublefome thoughts: we touch the land: the light of my days fhall in a moment diffipate the darknefs which furrounds me.

LETTER X.

I AM at laft arrived at this land, the objeƐt of my defires: but my dear *Aza*, I do not yet fee any thing, that confers the happinefs I had promifed myfelf: every objeƐt ftrikes, furprizes, aftonifhes, and leaves on me only a vague impreffion, and ftupid perplexity, which I do not attempt to throw off. My errors deftroy my judgment; I remain uncertain, and almoft doubt of what I behold.

Scarce were we got out of the floating houfe, but we entered a town built on the fea fhore. The people, who followed us in crowds, appeared to be of the fame nation as the *Cacique*: and the houfes did not at all refemble thofe of the cities of the Sun: but if thefe furpafs in beauty, by the richnefs of their ornaments, thofe are to be preferred, on account of the prodigies with which they are filled.

Upon entering the room affigned me by *Deterville*, my heart leaped: I faw fronting the door, a young perfon dreffed like a virgin of the Sun, and ran to her with open arms. How great was my furprize to find nothing but an impenetrable refiftance where I faw a human figure move in a very extended fpace!

Aftonifhment held me immoveable, with my eyes fixed upon this objeƐt, when *Deterville* made
me

me obferve his own figure on the fide of that which
engaged all my attention; I touched him, I fpoke
to him, and I faw him at the fame time very near
and very far from me.

Thefe prodigies confound reafon, and blind the
judgment. What ought we to think of the inhabitants of this country? Should we fear, or fhould
we love them? I will not take upon me to come to
any determination upon fo nice a fubject.

The *Cacique* made me underftand, that the figure which I faw was my own! But what information does that give me? Does it make the wonder
lefs great? Am I the lefs mortified to find nothing
but error and ignorance in my mind? With grief
I fee it, my dear *Aza*; the leaft knowing in this
country are wifer than all our *Amutas*.

The *Cacique* has given me a young and very
fprightly *China* *, and it affords me great pleafure
to fee a woman again, and to be ferved by her.
Many others of my fex wait upon me; but I had
rather they would let it alone, for their prefence
awakens my fears. One may fee, by their manner of looking on me, that they have never been
at *Cuzco* †. However, as my fpirit floats continually in a fea of uncertainties, I can judge of
nothing. My heart, alone unfhaken, defires, ex-
pects, waits for one happinefs only, without which
all the reft is pain and vexation.

LETTER XI.

THOUGH I have taken all the pains in my
power to gain fome light with refpect to my
prefent fituation, I am no better informed at this
inftant than I was three days ago. All that I have

been

* A maid fervant or chambermaid.
† The capital of *Peru*.

been able to obferve is, that the other favages of
this country appear as good and as humane as the
Cacique. They fing and dance, as if they had lands
to cultivate every day *. If I was to form a judgment from the oppofition of their cuftoms to thofe
of our nation, I fhould not have the leaft hope :
but I remember that thy auguft father fubjected to
his obedience provinces very remote, the people
of which had nothing in common with us. Why
may not this be one of thofe provinces? The fun
feems pleafed to enlighten it, and his beams are
more bright and pure than I ever faw them ‡.
This infpires me with confidence, and I am uneafy
only to think how long it muft be before I can be
fully informed of what regards our interefts : for,
my dear *Aza,* I am very certain that the knowledge of the language of the country will be fufficient to teach me the truth, and allay my inquietudes.

I let flip no opportunity of learning it, and avail
myfelf of all the moments wherein *Deterville*
leaves me at liberty, to take the inftructions of my
China. Little fervice indeed they do me ; for, as
I cannot make her underftand my thoughts, we
can hold no converfation, and I learn only the
names of fuch objects as ftrike both our fights.
The figns of the *Cacique* are fometimes more ufeful to me : cuftom has made it a kind of language
betwixt us, which ferves us at leaft to exprefs our
wills. He conducted me yefterday into a houfe,
where, without this knowledge, I fhould have be-
haved very ill.

We

* The lands in *Peru* are cultivated in common, and
the days they are about this work, are always days of
rejoicing.
‡ The fun never fhines clear in *Peru.*

We entered into a larger and better furnished apartment than that which I inhabit, and a great many people were there assembled. The general astonishment shewn at my appearance displeased me, and the excessive laughter which some young women endeavoured to stifle, but which burst out again, when they cast their eyes on me, gave me such uneasiness of mind, that I should have taken it for shame, if I could have found myself conscious of any fault: but, finding nothing within me but a repugnance to stay in such company, I was going to return back, when I was detained by a sign of *Deterville*.

I found that I should commit a fault by going out, and I took great care not to deserve the blame that was thrown on me without cause. As I fixed my attention, during my stay, upon those women, I thought I discovered that the singularity of my dress occasioned the surprize of some, and the laughter of others. I pitied their weakness, and endeavoured to persuade them by my countenance, that my soul did not so much differ from theirs, as my habit differed from their ornaments.

A young man, whom I should have taken for a *Curaca* *, if he had not been dressed in black, came and took me by the hand with an affable air, and led me to a woman, whom, by her haughty mien, I took for the *Pallas* † of the country. He spoke several words to her, which I remember by having heard *Deterville* pronounce the same a thousand times. *What a beauty!—What fine eyes! Aye*, answered another man, *she has the graces and the shape of a nymph.*

C 4

Except

---

* The *Curacas* were petty sovereigns of a country, who had the privilege of wearing the same dress as the *Incas*.

† A general name of the *Indian* princesses.

Except the women, who faid nothing, they all repeated almoft the fame words : I do not yet know their fignification ; but furely they exprefs agreeable ideas, for the countenance is always fmiling when they are pronounced.

The *Cacique* feems to be extremely well fatisfied with what they fay. He keeps clofe to me, or, if he fteps a little from me to fpeak to any one, his eyes are conftantly upon me, and he fhews me by figns what I am to do. For my part, I obferve him very attentively, as I would not offend againft the cuftoms of a people who know fo little of ours.

I believe, my dear *Aza*, I can fcarcely make thee comprehend how extraordinary the manners of thefe favages appear to me. They have fo impatient a vivacity, that words do not fuffice them for expreffion ; but they fpeak as much by the motion of the body as by the found of the voice. What I fee of their continual agitation, has fully convinced me how little importance there was in that behaviour of the *Cacique* which caufed me fo much uneafinefs, and upon which I made fo many falfe conjectures.

Yefterday he kiffed the hands of the *Pallas*, and of all the other women : nay, what I never faw before, he even kiffed their cheeks. The men came to embrace him ; fome took him by the hand; others pulled him by the clothes ; all with a fprightlinefs of which we have no idea.

The judge of their minds by the vivacity of their geftures, I am fure that our meafured expreffions, the fublime comparifons which fo naturally convey our tender fentiments and affectionate thoughts, would to them appear infipid. They would take our ferious and modeft air for ftupidity, and the gravity of our gait for mere ftiffnefs. Would'ft thou believe it, my dear *Aza ?* if thou wert here,

I could

I could be pleafed to live amongft them. A certain air of affability, fpread over all they do, renders them amiable ; and, if my foul was more happy, I fhould find a pleafure in the diverfity of objects that fucceffively pafs before my eyes : but the little reference they have to thee effaces the agreeablenefs of their novelty : thou alone art my good, and my pleafure.

LETTER XII.

I Have been long, my dear *Aza*, without being able to beftow a moment on my favourite occupation : yet I have a great many extraordinary things to communicate to thee, and avail myfelf of this firft fhort leifure to begin thy information.

The next day after I had vifited the *Pallas*, *Deterville* caufed a very fine habit, of the fafhion of the country, to be brought me. After my little *China* had put it on according to her fancy, fhe led me to that ingenious machine which doubles objects. Though I fhould be now habituated to its effects, I could not help being furprized at feeing my figure ftand as if I was over-againft myfelf.

My new accoutrements did not difpleafe me. Perhaps I fhould have more regretted thofe which I left off, if they had not made every body troublefome by their ftaring at me.

The *Cacique* came into my chamber, juft as the girl was adding fome trinkets to my drefs. He ftopped at the door, and looked at me for fome time without fpeaking. So profound was his reverence, that he ftept afide to let the *China* go out, and inadvertently put himfelf in her place. His eyes were fixed upon me, and he examined all my perfon with fuch a ferious attention as a little dif-

compofed

compofed me, though I knew not the reafon of what he did.

However, to fhew him my acknowledgmentfor his new benefactions, I offered him my hand, and, not being able to exprefs my fentiments, I thought I could not fay any thing more agreeable to him than fome of thofe words which he amufed himfelf with teaching me to repeat : I endeavoured even to give them the fame tone as he did in pronunciation.

What effect they inftantaneoufly had on him I know not : but his eyes fparkled, his cheeks reddened, he approached me trembling, and feemed to have a defire to fnatch me into his arms : then ftopping fuddenly he preffed my hand, and pronounced in a paffionate tone—*No—refpect—her virtue*—and many other words which I underftood no better than thefe. Then throwing himfelf upon his feat, on the other fide of the room, he leaned his head upon his hand, and fat mopeing with all the fymptoms of afflictive pain.

I was alarmed at his condition, not doubting but I had occafioned him fome uneafinefs : I drew near him to teftify my repentance ; but he gently pufhed me away without looking at me, and I did not dare fay any thing more. I was in the greateft confufion when the fervants came in to bring us victuals : he then rofe, and we eat together in our ufual manner, his pain feeming to have no other confequence but a little forrow : yet he was not lefs kind and good to me, which feemed to me inconceivable.

I did not dare to lift up my eyes upon him, or make ufe of the figns which commonly ferved us inftead of converfation : but our meal was at a time fo different from the ufual hour of repaft, that I could not help fhewing fome tokens of furprize.

All

All that I could underftand of his anfwer was, that we were foon to change our dwelling. In effect, the *Cacique*, after going in and out feveral times, came and took me by the hand. I let him lead me, ftill mufing with myfelf on what had paffed, and confidering whether the change of our place was not a confequence of it.

Scarce was I got without the outward door of the houfe, before he helped me up a pretty high ftep, and I advanced into a chamber fo low that one could not ftand upright in it: but there was room enough for the *Cacique*, the *China* and myfelf all to fit at eafe. This little apartment is agreeably decorated, has a window on each fide that enlightens it fufficiently; but it is not fpacious enough to walk in.

While I was confidering it with furprize, and endeavouring to divine what could be *Det rville*'s reafon for fhutting us up fo clofe (O my dear *Aza!* how familiar prodigies are in this country) I felt this machine, or cabin I know not what to call it, move and change its place. This motion made me think of the floating houfe. The *Cacique* faw me frightened, and, as he is attentive to my leaft uneafinefs, pacified me by making me look out of one of the windows. I faw, not without extreme furprize, that this machine, fufpended pretty near the earth, moved by a fecret power which I did not comprehend.

Deterville then fhewed me that feveral *Hamas**, of a fpecies unknown to us, went before us, and drew us after them. O light of my days! thefe people muft have a genius more than human that enables them to invent things fo ufeful and fingular: but there muft be alfo in this nation fome great defects

---

* A general name for beafts.

fects that moderate its power, otherwife it muft
needs be miftrefs of the whole world.

For four days we were fhut up in this wonderful machine, leaving it only at night to take our
reft in the firft houfe we came to; and then I
always quitted it with regret. I confefs, my dear
Aza, that, notwithftanding my tender inquietudes,
I have tafted pleafures, during this journey, that
were before unknown to me. Shut up in the temple from my moft tender infancy, I was unacquaint-
ed with the beauties of the univerfe, and every
thing that I fee ravifhes and enchants me.

The immenfe fields, which are inceffantly
changed and renewed, hurry on the attentive mind
with more rapidity than we pafs over them.

The eyes, without being fatigued, rove at once
over an infinite variety of admirable objects, and
at the fame time are at reft. One feems to find
no other bounds to the fight than thofe of the world
itfelf ; which error flatters us, gives us a fatisfac-
tory idea of our own grandeur, and feems to bring
us nearer to the creator of thefe wonders.

At the end of a fine day, the heavens prefent
to us a fpectacle not lefs admirable than that of
the earth. Tranfparent clouds affembled round
the fun, tinctured with the moft lively colours,
fhew us mountains of fhade and light in every part,
and the majeftic diforder attracts our admiration
till we forget ourfelves.

The *Cacique* has had the complaifance to let me
every day ftep out of the rolling cabbin, in order
to contemplate at leifure the wonders which he faw
me admire.

How delicious are the woods, my dear *Aza!*
If the beauties of heaven and earth tranfport us
far from ourfelves by an involuntary rapture, thofe
of the forefts bring us back again by an inward

in-

incomprehenfible bias, the fecret of which is in nature only. When we enter thefe delightful places, an univerfal charm overflows all the fenfes, and confound their ufe. We think we fee the cooling breeze before we feel it. The different fhades in the colour of leaves, foften the light that penetrates them, and feem to ftrike the fentiment as foon as the fight. An agreeable, but indeterminate odour, leaves it difficult for us to difcern whether it affects the tafte or the fmell. Even the air, without being perceived, conveys to our bodies a pure pleafure, which feems to give us another fenfe, though it does not mark out the organ of it.

O, my dear *Aza!* how would thy prefence embellifh thofe pure delights! how have I defired to fhare them with thee! Wert thou the witnefs of my tender thoughts, I fhould make thee find, in the fentiments of my heart, charms more powerful than all thofe of the beauties of the univerfe.

LETTER XIII.

AT laft, my dear *Aza*, I am got into a city called *Paris:* Our journey is at an end; but, according to all appearances, fo are not my troubles.

More attentive than ever, fince my arrival here, to all that paffes, my difcoveries produce only torment, and prefage nothing but misfortunes. I find thy idea in the leaft curious of my defires, but cannot meet with it in any of the objects that I fee.

As well as I can judge by the time we fpent in paffing through this city, and by the great number of inhabitants with whom the ftreets are filled, it contains more people than could be got together in two or three of our countries.

I reflect on the wonders that have been told me
of

of *Quito*, and endeavour to find here fome ftrokes of the picture which I conceive of that great city: But alas ! what a difference ?

This place contains bridges, rivers, trees, fields: it feems to be an univerfe, rather than a particular feat of habitation. I fhould endeavour in vain to give thee a juft idea of the height of the houfes. They are fo prodigioufly elevated, that it is more eafy to believe nature produced them as they are, than to comprehend how men could build them.

Here it is that the family of the *Cacique* refides. Their houfe is almoft as magnificent as that of the Sun : the furniture and fome parts of the walls are of gold, and the reft is adorned with a various mixture of the fineft colours, which prettily enough reprefent the beauties of nature.

At my arrival, *Deterville* made me underftand that he was conducting me to his mother's apartment. We found her reclined upon a bed of almoft the fame form with that of the *Incas*, and of the fame metal *. After having held out her hand to the *Cacique*, who kiffed it bowing almoft to the ground, fhe embraced him ; but with a kindnefs fo cold, a joy fo conftrained, that, if previous information had not been given me, I fhould not have known the fentiments of nature in the careffes of this mother.

After a moment's converfation, the *Cacique* made me draw near. She caft on me a difdainful look, and, without anfwering what her fon faid to her, continued gravely to turn round her finger a thread, which hung to a fmall piece of gold.

Deterville left us to go and meet a ftately, bulky man, who has advanced fome fteps towards him.

He

---

* The beds, chairs, and tables of the *Incas* were of maffy gold.

He embraced both him and a woman who was employed in the fame manner as the *Pallas*.

As foon as the *Cacique* had appeared in the chamber, a young maiden, of about my age, ran to us, and followed him with a timed eagernefs that feemed remarkable. Joy fhone upon her countenance, yet did not banifh the marks of a forrow that feemed to affect her. *Deterville* embraced her laft, but with a tendernefs fo natural, that my heart was moved at it. Alas! my dear *Aza*, what would our tranfports be, if after fo many misfortunes, fate fhould reunite us?

During this time I kept near the *Pallas*, whom I durft not quit, nor look up at *, out of refpect. Some fevere glances, which fhe threw from time to time upon me, compleated my confufion, and put me under a conftraint that affected my very thoughts.

At laft, the young damfel, as if fhe had gueffed at my diforder, as foon as fhe had quitted *Deterville*, came and took me by the hand, and led me to a window where we both fat down. Though I did not underftand any thing fhe faid to me, her eyes full of goodnefs fpoke to me the univerfal language of beneficent hearts; they infpired me with a confidence and friendfhip which I would willingly have expreffed to her? but not being able to utter the fentiments of my mind, I pronounced all that I knew of her language.

She fmiled more than once, looking on *Detterville* with the moft tender fweetnefs. I was pleafing myfelf with this converfation, when the *Pallas* fpoke fome words aloud, looking fternly on my new friend; whofe countenance immediately falling, fhe truft

---

* Young damfels, though of the blood royal, fhow a profound refpect to married women.

truft away my hand which fhe before held in hers, and took no farther notice of me.

Some time after that, an old woman of gloomy appearance, entered the room, went up towards the *Pallas*, then came and took me by the arm, led me to a chamber at the top of the houfe, and left me there alone.

Though this moment could not be efteemed the moft unfortunate of my life, yet my dear *Aza*, I could not pafs it without much concern. I expected, at the end of my journey, fome relief to my fatigues, and that in the *Cacique*'s family I fhould at leaft meet with the fame kindnefs as from him. The cold reception of the *Pallas*, the fudden change of behaviour in the damfel, the rudenefs of this woman in forcing me from a place where I had rather have ftaid, the inattention of *Deterville*, who did not oppofe the violence fhewn me; in a word, all circumftances that might augment the pains of an unhappy mind, prefented themfelves at once with their moft rueful afpects! I thought myfelf abandoned by all the world, and was bitterly deploring my difmal deftiny, when I beheld my *China* coming in. Her prefence, in my fituation, feemed to me an effential good: I ran to her, embraced her with tears, and was more melted when I faw her touched with my affliction. When a mind is reduced to pity itfelf, the compaffion of another is very valuable. The marks of this young woman's affection foftened my anguifh: I related to her my griefs, as if fhe could underftand me: I afked her a thoufand queftions, as if it had been in her power to anfwer them. Her tears fpoke to my heart, and mine continued to flow, but with lefs bitternefs than before.

I thought, at leaft, that I fhould fee *Deterville* at the hour of refrefhment; but they brought me up
victuals,

victuals, and I faw him not. Since I have loft thee, dear idol of my heart, this *Cacique* is the only human creature that has fhewn me an uninterrupted courfe of goodnefs: fo that the cuftom of feeing him became a kind of neceffity. His abfence redoubled my forrow. After expecting him long in vain, I laid me down; but fleep had not yet fealed my eyes before I faw him enter my chamber, followed by the young woman whofe brifk difdain had fo fenfibly afflicted me.

She threw herfelf upon my bed, and by a thoufand careffes feemed defirous to repair the ill treatment fhe had given me.

The *Cacique* fat down by my bedfide, and feemed to receive as much pleafure in feeing me again, as I enjoyed in perceiving I was not abandoned. They talked together with their eyes fixed on me, and heaped on me the moft tender marks of affection.

Infenfibly their converfation became more ferious. Though I did not underftand their difcourfe, it was eafy for me to judge that it was founded on confidence and friendfhip. I took care not to interrupt them: but, as foon as they returned to my bedfide, I endeavoured to obtain from the *Cacique* fome light with regard to thofe particulars which had appeared to me the moft extraordinary fince my arrival.

All that I could underftand from his anfwers was, that the name of the young woman before me was *Celina*; that fhe was his fifter; that the great man, whom I had feen in the chamber of the *Pallas*, was his elder brother, and the other young woman, that brother's wife.

Celina became more dear to me, when I underftood fhe was the *Cacique*'s fifter, and the company

ny

ny of both was fo agreeable, that I did not perceive it was day light before they left me.

After their departure, I fpent the reft of the time, deftined to repofe, in thus converfing with thee. This is my happinefs, my only joy : It is to thee alone, dear foul of my thoughts, that I unbofom my heart; thou fhalt ever be the fole depofitory of my fecrets, my paffions, and my fentiments.

LETTER XIV.

IF I did not continue, my dear *Aza*, to take from my fleep the time that I give to thee, I fhould no more enjoy thofe delicious moments in which I exift for thee only. They have made me refume my virgin habits, and oblige me to remain all day in a room full of people, who are changed and renewed every moment without feeming to diminifh.

This involuntary diffipation, in fpite of me, often caufes a fufpenfion of my tender thoughts: but if, for fome moments, I lofe that lively attention which unites our hear.s, I always find thee again in the advantageous comparifons I make of thee with whatever furrounds me.

In the different countries that I have paffed through, I have not feen any favages fo haughtily familiar as thefe. The women, in particular, feem to have a kind of difdainful civility that difgufts human nature, and would perhaps infpire me with as much contempt for them, as they fhew for others, if I knew them better.

One of them caufed an affront to be given me yefterday, which ftill afflicts me. Juft when the affembly was moft numerous, after fhe had been fpeaking to feveral perfons without perceiving me; whether by chance, or that fomebody made her
take

take notice of me; as soon as she cast her eyes on me, she burst out a laughing, quitted her place precipitately, came to me, made me rise, and after having turned me backwards and forwards, as often as her vivacity prompted, after having handled all the parts of my dress with a scrupulous attention, she beckoned to a young man to draw near, and began again with him the examination of my figure.

Though I shewed a dislike to the liberty which both of them took, as the richness of the woman's dress made me take her for a *Pallas,* and the magnificence of the young man, who was all over plated with gold, made him look like an *Anqui* *, I dared not oppose their will: but this rash savage, emboldened by the familiarity of the *Pallas,* and perhaps by my submission, having had the impudence to put his hand upon my neck, I pushed it away with a surprize and indignation that shewed him I understood good manners better than himself.

Upon my crying out, *Deterville* came up, and after he had spoke a few words to the young savage, the latter, clapping one hand upon his shoulder, set up such a laugh as quite distorted his figure.

The *Cacique* disengaged himself, and, blushing, spoke to him in so cold a tone, that the young man's gaiety vanished: he seemed to have no more to say, and retired without coming near us again.

O my dear *Aza,* what a respect do the manners of this couutry make me have for those of the children of the Sun! How does the temerity of the young *Anqui* bring back to my mind thy tender respect, thy sage reserve, and the charms of decency that

* A prince of the blood. There must be leave from an *Inca* for a *Peruvian* to wear gold upon his apparel, and the *Inca* gives this permission only to the princes of the blood royal.

that reigned in our converfations! I perceived it the
firft moment I faw thee, dear delight of my foul,
and I fhall think of it all the days of my life. Thou
alone uniteft in thyfelf all the perfections which nature has fhed upon mankind; as my heart has collected within it all the fentiments of tendernefs
and admiration that will attach me to thee till
death.

LETTER XV.

THE more I fee the *Cacique* and his fifter, my
dear *Aza*, the more difficulty I have to perfuade myfelf that they are of this nation: they alone
know what virtue is, and refpect it.

The fimple manners, the native goodnefs, and
the modeft gaiety of *Celina*, would make one think
fhe had been bred up among our virgins. The
honeft fweetnefs, the ferious tendernefs of her brother, would eafily perfuade me that he was born
of the blood of the *Incas*. They both treat me with
as much humanity as we fhould fhew them, if like
misfortunes had brought them among us.

I do not doubt but the *Cacique* is a good tribu-
tary *.

He never enters my apartment but he makes me
a prefent of fome of the wonderful things with
which this country abounds. Sometimes they are
pieces of that machine which doubles objects, enclofed in little frames of curious matter. At other
times he brings me little ftones of furprifing luftre,
with which it is the cuftom here to adorn almoft
all

* The *Caciques* and *Curacas* were obliged to furnifh the
drefs and provifions of the *Inca* and the queen. They never
came into the prefence of either, without offering them
fome tribute of the curiofities of the province they commanded.

all the parts of the body: they hang them to their ears, put them on the stomach, the neck, the knees, and even the shoes; all which has a very agreeable effect.

But what I am most amused with are certain small utensils of a very hard metal, and most singular use. Some are employed in the works which *Celina* teaches me to make: others, of a cutting form, serve to divide all sorts of stuffs, of which we make as many bits as we please without trouble, and in a very ingenious, diverting manner.

I have an infinite number of other rarities still more extraordinary: which not being in use with us, I cannot find words in our tongue to give thee an idea of them.

I keep all these gifts carefully for thee, my dear *Aza*: besides the pleasure thy surprize will give me when thou seest them, they undoubtedly belong to thee. If the *Cacique* was not subject to thy obedience, would he pay me a tribute which he knows to be due only to thy supreme rank? The respect he has always shewn me, made me think from the first, that my birth was known to him; and the presents he now honours me with convince me that he knows I am to be thy spouse, since he treats me already as a *Mama Oella* *.

This conviction revives me, and calms a part of my inquietudes. I conceive that nothing is wanting but the power of expressing myself, for me to be informed what are the *Cacique's* reasons for keeping me, and to determine him to deliver me into thy power: but, till that can be, I have a great many pains to suffer.

The humour of *Madame* (so they call *Deterville's* mother)

* This is the name the queens take when they ascend the throne.

mother) is not near so amiable as that of her children. Far from treating me with so much goodnefs, fhe fhews me on all occafions a coldnefs and difdain that mortifies me, though I can neither remedy nor difcover the caufe of it; and yet, by an oppofition of fentiments that I underftood ftill lefs, fhe requires to have me continually with her.

This gives me infupportable torture; for conftraint reigns wherever fhe is, and it is only by ftealth that *Celina* and her brother give me figns of their friendfhip. They do not themfelves dare to fpeak freely before her: for which reafon they fpend part of the nights in my chamber, which is the only time we enjoy in peace the pleafure of feeing one another. Though I cannot partake of their converfation, their prefence is always agreeable to me. It is not for want of care in either of them that I am not happy. Alas! my dear *Aza*, they are ignorant that I cannot bear to be remote from thee, and that I do not think myfelf to live, except when the remembrance of thee, and my tendernefs employ me entirely.

LETTER XVI.

I HAVE fo few *Quipos* left, my dear *Aza*, that I fcarce dare ufe them. When I would go to knotting them, the dread of feeing an end of them ftops me; as if I could multiply by fparing them. I am going to lofe the pleafure of my foul, the fupport of my life: nothing can relieve the weight of thy abfence, which muft now weigh me down.

I tafted a delicate pleafure in preferving the remembrance of the moft fecret motions of my heart to offer thee its homage. My defign was to preferve the memory of the principal cuftoms of this fingular nation, to amufe thy leifure with in more

happy

happy times. Alas! I have little hopes now left of executing my project.

If I find at prefent fo much difficulty in putting my ideas into order, how fhall I hereafter recall them without foreign affiftance? 'Tis true they offer me one; but the execution of it is fo difficult, that I think it impoffible.

The *Cacique* has brought me one of this country favages, who comes daily to give me leffons in his tongue, and to fhew me the method of giving a fort of exiftence to thoughts. This is done by drawing fmall figures, which they call *Letters*, with a feather upon a thin matter called *Paper*. Thefe figures have names, and thofe names put together reprefent the found of words. But thefe names and founds feem to me fo little diftinct from one another, that if I do in time fucceed in learning them, I am fure it will not be without a great deal of pains. This poor favage takes an incredible deal to teach me, and I give myfelf more to learn: yet I make fo little progrefs, that I would renounce the enterprize, if I knew any other way to inform myfelf of thy fate and mine.

There is no other, my dear *Aza*; therefore my whole delight is now in this new and fingular ftudy. I would live alone: all that I fee difpleafes me, and the neceffity impofed on me of being always in *Madame*'s apartment, gives me great torment.

At firft, by exciting the curiofity of others, I amufed my own: but, where the eyes only are to be ufed, they are foon to be fatisfied. All the women are alike, have ftill the fame manners, and I think they always fpeak the fame words. The appearances are more varied among the men: fome of them look as if they thought: but in general, I fufpect this nation not to be what it appears: for affectation feems to be its ruling character.

If

If the demonftrations of zeal and earneftnefs, with which the moft trifling duties of fociety are here graced, were natural, thefe people, my dear *Aza*, muft certainly have in their hearts more goodnefs and humanity than ours: and who can think this poffible?

If they had as much ferenity in the foul as upon the countenance, if the propenfity to joy, which I remark in all their actions, was fincere, would they chufe for their amufement fuch fpectacles as they have carried me to fee?

They conducted me into a place, where was reprefented, almoft as in thy palace, the actions of men who are no * more. But as we revive only the memory of the moft wife and virtuous, I believe only madmen and villains are reprefented here. Thofe who perfonated them raved and ftormed as if they were wild; and I faw one of them carry his fury fo high as to kill himfelf. The fine women, whom feemingly they perfecuted, wept inceffantly, and fhewed fuch tokens of defpair, that the words they made ufe of were not neceffary to fhew the excefs of their anguifh.

Could one think, my dear *Aza*, that a whole people, whofe outfide is fo humane, fhould be pleafed at the reprefentation of thofe misfortunes or crimes, which either overwhelmed or degraded creatures like themfelves?

But perhaps they have occafion here for the horror of vice to conduct them to virtue. This thought ftarts upon me unfought; and if it were true, how fhould I pity fuch a nation? Ours, more favoured by nature, cherifhes goodnefs for its own charms; we want only models of virtue to make us virtuous;

as

* The *Incas* caufed a kind of comedies to be reprefented, the fubjects of which were taken from the brighteft actions of their predeceffors.

as nothing is requifite but to love thee in order to become amiable.

LETTER XVII.

I Know not what farther to think of the genius of this nation, my dear *Aza*. It runs through the extreams with fuch rapidity, that it requires more ability than I poffefs to fit in judgment upon its chara&er.

They have fhewn me a fpe&acle intirely oppo-fite to the former. That, cruel and frightful, made reafon revolt, and humbled humanity: this amufing and agreeable, imitates nature, and does honour to good fenfe. It was compofed of a great many more men and women than the former: they repre-fented alfo fome a&ions of human life; but whether they expreffed pain or pleafure, joy or forrow, the whole was done by fongs and dances.

The intelligence of founds, my dear *Aza*, muft be univerfal: for I found it no more difficult to be affe&ed with the different paffions that were re-prefented, than if they had been expreffed in our language. This feems to me very natural.

Human fpeech is doubtlefs of man's invention, becaufe it differs according to the difference of nati-ons. Nature, more powerful, and more attentive to the neceffities and pleafures of her creatures, has given them general means of expreffing them, which are well imitated by the fongs I heard.

If it be true that fharp founds exprefs better the need of help, in violent fear, or acute pain, than words underftood in one part of the world, and which have no fignification in another; it is not lefs certain that the tender fighs ftrike our hearts with a more efficacious compaffion than words, the odd

D   ftrange.

arrangement of which fometimes produces juft a contrary effect.

Do not lively and light founds inevitably excite in our foul that gay pleafure, which the recital of a diverting ftory, or a joke properly introduced, can but imperfectly raife.

Are there expreffions in any language that can communicate genuine pleafure with fo much fuccefs as the natural fports of animals? Dancing feems an humble imitation of them, and infpires much the fame fentiment.

In fhort, my dear *Aza*, every thing in this laft fhow was comformable to nature and humanity. Can any benefit be conferred on man, equal to that of infpiring him with joy?

I felt it myfelf, and was tranfported by it in fpite of me, when I was interrupted by an accident that happened to *Celina*.

As we came out, we ftep'd a little afide from the crowd, and lean'd on one another for fear of falling. *Deterville* was fome paces before us leading his fifter-in-law, when a young favage of an amiable figure, came up to *Celina*, whifpered a few words to her very low; gave her a bit of paper, which fhe fcarce had ftrength to take, and retired.

Celina, who was fo frightened at his approach as to make me partake of her trembling, turned her head languifhingly towards him when he quitted us. She feemed fo weak, that, fearing fhe was attacked by fome fudden illnefs, I was going to call *Deterville* to her affiftance: but fhe ftop'd me, and, by putting her finger on her mouth, required me to be filent. I chofe rather to be uneafy, than to difobey her.

The fame evening, when the brother and fifter came into my chamber, *Celina* fhewed the *Cacique* the paper fhe had received. By the little I could

guefs

guefs at in their converfation, I fhoud have thought
fhe loved the young man who gave it her, if it had
been poffible for one to be frightned at the prefence
of what one loves.

I have made other remarks, my dear *Aza*, which
I would have imparted to thee: but alas! my *Quipos* are all ufed; the laft threads are in my hands,
and I am knotting the laft knots. The knots,
which feemed to me a chain of communication
betwixt my heart and thine, are now only the forrowful objects of my regret. Illufion quits me;
frightful truth takes her place; my wandering
thoughts, bewildered in the immence void of abfence, will hereafter be annihilated with the fame
rapidity as time. Dear *Aza*, they feem to feparate
us once again, and fnatch me afrefh from thy love.
I lofe thee! I quit thee! I fhall fee thee no more!
Aza, dear hope of my heart, how diftant indeed
are we now to be removed from each other!

LETTER XVIII.

HOW much of my time has been effaced, my
dear *Aza*! The Sun has run half his courfe
fince I laft enjoyed the artificial happinefs of believing I converfed with thee. How tedious has this dou-
ble abfence appeared! What courage did I want to
fupport it! I lived in futurity only, and the prefent
time did not feem worthy to be computed. All my
thoughts were nothing but defires, my reflections
but fo many projects, and my fentiments but a feries of hopes.

Scarce have I learned to form thefe figures, and
yet I will try to make them the interpreters of my
paffion.

I feel myfelf reanimated by this amiable employment: reftored to myfelf, I begin to live again. *Aza*,

how

how dear art thou! what delight do I take in telling thee fo, in painting thefe fentiments, and giving them all poffible means of exiftence! I would trace them upon the hardeft metal, upon the walls of my chamber, upon my garments, upon all that fur- rounds me, and exprefs them in all languages.

How fatal, alas, has the knowledge of the lan- guage I now ufe been to me! How deceitful was the hope that prevailed on me to learn it! Scarce had I got acquainted with it but a new univerfe opened to my eye; objects took another form, and every light I gained difcovered to me a new mif- fortune.

My mind, my heart, my eyes, the Sun him- felf has deceived me. He enlightens the whole world, of which thy empire, and the various king- doms that own thy fupremacy, are a portion only. Do not think, my dear *Aza*, that they have impo- fed upon me in thefe incredible facts, which they have but too well proved.

Far from being among people fubjected to thy obedience, I am not only under foreign dominion, but fo prodigioufly remote from thy empire, that our nation had ftill been unknown here, if the ava- rice of the *Spaniards* had not made them furmount the moft hideous dangers to come at us.

Will not love do as much as thirft of riches has done? If thou loveft me, if thou defireft me, if thou only thinkeft yet of the unhappy *Zilia*, I have every thing to expect from thy tendernefs and thy generofity. Let them teach me the roads that lead to thee, and the perils to be furmounted, or the fatigues to be borne, fhall be fo many pleafures to my paffionate heart.

LETTER XIX.

I AM as yet fo very imperfect in the art of writing, that it takes me up abundance of time to form only a few lines. Often it happens, my dear *Aza*, that, after having written much, I cannot myself divine what I have endeavoured to exprefs. This perplexity confounds my ideas, and makes me forget what I had with pain revolved in my memory. I begin again, do no better, and yet I proceed.

The talk would be more eafy to me, if I had nothing to give thee but expreffions of my tendernefs: the vivacity of my fentiments would then furmount all difficulties.

But I would alfo render thee an account of all that has paffed during the long interval of my filence. I would not have thee ignorant of any of my actions: and yet of fo little importance, fo little uniform have they a long time been, that it would be impoffible for me to diftinguifh one from another.

The principal event of my life has been *Deterville*'s departure.

As long ago as they call here *fix months*, he has been gone to war for the intereft of his fovereign. When he fet out, I did not then know his language: but, by the lively grief he difcovered at parting from his fifter and me, I underftood that we were going to lofe him for a long time.

I fhed many tears; a thoufand fears filled my heart, left the kindnefs of *Celina* fhould wear off. In him I loft the moft folid hope of feeing thee again. To whom could I have had recourfe, if any new misfortunes had happened to me? Nobody underftood my language.

It

It was not long before I felt the effects of this abſence. *Madame*, his mother, whoſe contempt I had but too juſtly gueſſed at (and who had not kept me ſo much in her chamber, but to indulge the vanity ſhe conceived on account of my birth, and the power ſhe had over me) cauſed me to be ſhut up with *Celina* in a houſe of virgins, where we now are. The life that we lead here is ſo very uniform, that it can produce but inconſiderable events.

This retreat would not diſpleaſe me if it had not deprived me (juſt as I began to be initiated) of the inſtructions I wanted to carry on my deſign of coming to thee. The virgins that live here are ſo profoundly ignorant, that they cannot ſatisfy my moſt trifling enquiries.

The worſhip which they render to the divinity of the country requires that they ſhould renounce all his benefits, all intelligence of the mind, all the ſentiments of the heart, and I think even reaſon itſelf, if one may judge from their diſcourſe.

Though ſhut up like ours, theſe virgins have one advantage that is not to be found in the temple of the Sun. The walls are open here in ſeveral places, and ſecured only by croſs bars of iron, ſo cloſe that they cannot be got between. By theſe places, which are called *Parlours*, they have the liberty of converſing with perſons who are without.

It is through one of theſe convenient places that I continue to have my writing leſſons. I ſpeak to nobody but the maſter who gives them to me; and his ignorance, in every thing but his art, is not like to reſcue me out of mine. *Celina* ſeems no better informed than the reſt: in the anſwers ſhe gives to my queſtions, I obſerve a certain perplexity, which can proceed from nothing put either aukward

aukward diffimulation, or profound ignorance. Which fover it be, her converfation is always confined to the affairs of her own heart, and thofe of her family.

The young *Frenchman*, who fpoke to her as we came out from the finging entertainment, is her lover, as I gueffed before.

But madame *Deterville*, who will not let them come together, forbids her feeing him; and, the more effectually to hinder her, will not permit her to fpeak to any perfon whatfoever without.

Not that the choice is unworthy of her, but this vain and unnatural mother, taking advantage of a barbarous cuftom eftablifhed among the great in this country, obliges *Celina* to put on the virgin's habit, in order to make her eldeft fon the richer.

From the fame motive fhe has obliged *Deter-ville* to enter into a particular order, from which he cannot be difengaged after he has pronounced certain words called *Vows.*

Celina, with all her power, oppofes the facrifice they would make of her: Her courage is fupported by her lover's letters, which I receive from my writing mafter, and deliver to her. Yet her vexation fo alters her character, that, far from fhewing me the fame kindnefs fhe did before I fpoke her tongue, fhe fpreads fuch a fournefs over all our converfation, as renders my forrows the more acute.

Her troubles, of which I am the perpetual confidante, I hear without difguft: I bewail them without art, and comfort her with friendfhip: but if my tendernefs, awakened by the picture of hers, drives me to feek eafe to my oppreffed heart by only pronouncing thy name, impatience and contempt are immediately painted in her countenance; fhe dif-

D 4

putes

putes thy underftanding, thy virtues, and even thy love.

My very *China* (I have no other name for her, this having fo pleafed that it has been continued) my *China*, who feemed to love me, who obeyed me in all things, takes the liberty to exhort me to think no more of thee, or leaves me, if I bid her be filent. *Celina* then comes in, and I muft hide my refentment.

This tyrannical conftraint heightens all my misfortunes. I have nothing left but the painful fatisfaction of covering this paper with expreffions of my tendernefs, it being the only docile witnefs of the fentiments of my heart.

Alas! perhaps the pains I take are ufelefs; perhaps thou wilt never know that I lived for thee alone. This horrible thought enfeebles my courage, yet does not interrupt my defign of continuing to write to thee. I preferve my illufion, that I may preferve my life for thee. I banifh the cruel reafon that would inform me. If I did not hope to fee thee again, I am fure, my dear *Aza*, I fhould perifh; for life without thee is a torment to me.

LETTER XX.

HITHERTO, my dear *Aza*, intent only about the afflictions of my heart, I have faid nothing to thee concerning thofe of my underftanding: yet thefe are not the lefs cruel, becaufe I have omitted them. I experience one of a kind unknown among us, and which nothing but the equivocal genius of this nation could invent.

The government of this empire, quite oppofite to that of thine, muft needs be defective. Whereas the *Capa Inca* is obliged to provide for the fubfiftence of his people, in *Europe* the fovereigns fubfift
only

only on the labours of their fubjects: whence it is that moft of the crimes and misfortunes proceed here from unfatisfied neceffities.

The misfortunes of the nobles in general, arife from the difficulties they are under to reconcile their apparent magnificence with their real mifery.

The common people fupport their condition by what is called commerce or induftry, the leaft evil arifing from which is infincerity.

Part of the people, in order to live, are obliged to depend on the humanity of others; and that is fo bounded, that fcarce have thofe wretches fufficient to keep them alive.

Without gold, it is impoffible to acquire any part of that land which nature has given in common to all men. Without poffeffing what they call wealth, it is impoffible to have gold; and, by a falfe confequence, repugnant to reafon and natural light, this fenfelefs people, thinking it a fhame to receive from any other than the fovereign the means of life, and the fupport of dignity, give that fovereign an opportunity of fhowering down his liberalities on fo fmall a number of his fubjects, in comparifon with thofe that are miferable, that there would be as much folly in pretending to any fhare in them, as there would be ignominy in obtaining deliverance by death from the impoffibility of living without fhame.

The knowledge of thefe woful truths excited in my heart at firft only pity for the miferable wretches, and indignation againft the laws. But alas! how many cruel reflections does the contemptuous manner, in which I hear them fpeak of thofe that are not rich, caufe me to make on myfelf! I have neither gold, nor land, nor addrefs, and yet I neceffarily make a part of the citizens of this

place.

place. O heaven ! in what clafs muft I rank myfelf ?

Though I am a ftranger to all fentiment of
fhame, which does not arife from a fault committed ; though I perceive how foolifh it is to blufh
for caufes independent of my power and my will ;
I cannot help fuffering from the idea which others
have of me. This pain would be infupportable to
me, if I did not hope that thy generofity will one
day put me in a condition to recompenfe thofe,
who, in fpite of me, humble me by benefits with
which I once thought myfelf honoured.

Not that *Celina* omits any thing in her power
to calm my inquietudes in this refpect : but what
I fee, what I learn of this country, gives me a
general diffidence of their words. Their virtues,
my dear *Aza*, have no more reality than their
riches. The moveables, which I thought were of
gold, have only a thin fuperficies of that metal,
their true fubftance being wood. In like manner
what they call *politenefs* has all the outward forms
of virtue, and lightly vails over their faults ; but,
with a little attention, the artifice of this is difcovered, as well as their falfe riches.

I owe part of this knowledge to a fort of writing
they call *books*. Though I found it every difficult
to comprehend what they contain, they have been
of great ufe to me : I extract notions from them ;
Celina explains to me what fhe knows, and I form
fuch ideas as I think are juft.

Some of thefe *books* teach me what men have
done, and others what they have thought. I cannot explain to thee, my dear *Aza*, the exquifite
pleafure I fhould take in reading them, if I did
but underftand them better ; nor the extreme defire I have to know fome of thofe divine men who
compofe them. As they are to the foul what the
fun

fun is to the earth, I fhould with them find all the
lights, all the helps I want : but I fee no hope of
ever having that fatisfaction. Though *Celina* reads
pretty often, fhe is not knowing enough to fatisfy
me. As if fhe had never reflected that books
were made by men, fhe is ignorant of their very
names, and feem not to have reflected that fuch
men ever lived.

I will convey to thee, my dear *Aza*, all that I
can collect from their wonderful works : I will
explain them in our language, and fhall tafte
fupreme felicity in giving a new pleafure to him I
love.

Alas ! fhall I ever be able to perform my promife ?

LETTER XXI.

I Shall not for the future want matter to entertain thee, my dear *Aza :* they have let me
fpeak to a *Cucipata*, whom they call a *religious
man*, who knows every thing, and has promifed
to leave me ignorant of nothing. As polite as a
great lord, as learned as an *Amutas*, he knows as
well the cuftoms of the world as the tenets of his
religion. His converfation, more ufeful than
a book, has given me a fatisfaction which I had
not tafted fince my misfortunes feparated me from
thee.

He came to teach me the religion of *France*,
and exhort me to embrace it : which I would
willingly have done, if I had been well affured
that he gave me a true picture of it.

According to what he faid to me of the virtues
it prefcribes, they are drawn from the law of
nature, and not lefs pure in fact than ours : but I
have not penetration enough to perceive here that

agreement,

agreement, which the manners and cuſtoms of a nation ſhould have with their religion: on the contrary, I find ſuch a want of connexion betwixt theſe, that my reaſon abſolutely refuſes to believe my inſtructor.

With regard to the origin and principles of this religion, they did not appear to me either more incredible, or more incompatible with good ſenſe, than the hiſtory of *Mancocapac* and the lake *Tiſicaca* * : I ſhould therefore have been ready to embrace it, if the *Cucipata* had not indignantly deſpiſed the worſhip which we render to the Sun. Partiality of any kind deſtroys confidence.

I might have applied to his arguments what he oppoſed to mine: but if the laws of humanity forbid to ſtrike another, becauſe it is doing him an injury, there is more reaſon why one ſhould not hurt the ſoul of another by a contempt of his opinions. I contented myſelf with explaining to him my ſentiments, but did not attempt to contradict his.

Beſides, a more dear concern preſſed me to change the ſubject of our converſation. I interrupted him as ſoon as poſſible, to aſk how far the city of *Paris* was from that of *Cuzco*; and whether it was poſſible to get from one to the other. The *Cucipata* ſatisfied me kindly; and though the diſtance he told me there was betwixt the two cities was enough to make me deſpair; though he made me look on the difficulty of performing this voyage as almoſt inſurmountable; it was ſufficient for me to know that the thing was poſſible, in order to confirm my courage, and give me confidence to communicate my deſign to the good father.

He ſeemed aſtoniſhed, and endeavoured to divert

* See the hiſtory of the *Incas*.

vert me from my project with such tender words,
that I was affected myself at hearing the dangers
I was to be exposed to : but my resolution however
was unshaken, and I prayed the *Cucipata*, in the
warmest manner, to teach me the means of returning into my country. He would not enter
into particulars, and only told me that *Deterville*,
by his high birth and personal merit, being in great
credit, might do what he would for me ; and that
having an uncle all powerful at the court of *Spain*,
he could more easily than any man procure me
news from our unhappy country.

The better to determine me to wait for his return (which he assured me to be near at hand) he
added, that, after the obligations I had to this
generous friend, I could not honourably dispose of
myself without his consent. I agreed with him,
and heard with pleasure the encomium he made of
those rare qualities, which distinguish *Deterville*
from those of his rank. The weight of acknowledgment is very light, my dear *Aza*, when one
receives favours only from the hands of virtue.

The learned man informed me also how chance
had conducted the *Spaniards* to thy unfortunate
empire, and that the thirst of gold was the sole
cause of their cruelty. He then explained to me
in what manner the rights of war had caused me
to fall into the hands of *Deterville*, by a fight in
which he was victorious, after having taken several
ships from the *Spaniards*, and among them that in
which I was embarked.

In fine, my dear *Aza*, if he has confirmed my
misfortunes, he has at least drawn me out of that
cruel darkness, in which I lived with regard to all
those extraordinary events. This is no small solace
to my pains, and for the rest I wait the return of
Deterville. He is humane, noble, virtuous, and
I may

I may depend upon his generofity. If he reftores
me to thee, what a benefit! what joy! what happinefs!—

LETTER XXII.

I Trufted, my dear *Aza*, upon making me a
friend of the learned *Cucipata* : but a fecond
vifit he has made me, has deftroyed the good opinion I formed of him in the firft: in fhort, we
have already differed.

If at firft he appeared to me gentle and fincere,
this time I found nothing but rudenefs and falfhood
in all that he faid to me.

My mind being eafy with regard to the objeƐ
of my tendernefs, I defired to fatisfy my curiofity
concerning the wonderful men who make books:
I began by enquiring what rank they held in the
world, what veneration was paid to them ; in fhort,
what were the honours and triumphs decreed to
them for fo many benefits beftowed on fociety.

I know not what pleafantry the *Cucipata* found
in my queftions, but he fmiled at each of them,
and anfwered me only by fuch broken fentences,
that it was not difficult for me to fee he deceived
me.

In faƐ, ought I to believe that perfons, who
know and paint fo well the fubtle delicacies of virtue,
fhould not have more, nay fhould fometimes have
lefs of it in their hearts than other men ? Can I
believe that intereft is the guide of a labour more
than human ; and that fo many pains are reward-
only by railleries, or at beft by a little money ?

Can I perfuade myfelf that, in fo haughty a
nation, men who are indifputably above others by
the light of their underftanding, are reduced to
the woful neceffity of felling their thoughts, as
people

people fell for bread the meaneft productions of the earth?

Falfhood, my dear *Aza*, does not lefs difpleafe me when under the tranfparent mafk of pleafantry, than when under the thick vail of feduction: that of the father provoked me, and I did not deign to give him an anfwer.

Not being able to fatisfy myfelf in this refpect, I turned the converfation again to. the project of my voyage; but, inftead of diffuading me from it with the fame gentlenefs as before, he oppofed fuch ftrong and convincing reafons againft me, that I had nothing but my paffion for thee to combat them with, and I·made 'no fcruple of confeffing as much.

At firft he affumed a gay air; and, feeming to doubt the truth of my words, anfwered only by jokes, which, infipid as they were, did not fail of offending me. I laboured to convince him of my truth; but, in proportion as the expreffions of my heart proved its fentiments, his countenance and words grew fevere. He dared to tell me that my love for thee was incompatible with virtue; that I muft renounce one or the other; in fhort, that I could not love thee without a crime.

At thefe fenfelefs words the moft violent wrath took poffeffion of my foul: I forgot the moderation I had prefcribed myfelf: I loaded him with reproaches: I told him what I thought of the falfity of his words: I protefted to him a thoufand times that I would love thee always; and, without waiting for his excufes, quitted him, and ran and fhut myfelf up in my chamber, whither I was fure he could not follow me.

O my dear *Aza!* how whimfical is the reafon of this country! Always in contradiction with itfelf,

I cannot

I cannot underſtand how I am to obey ſome of its precepts without thwarting many others.

It agrees in general that to do good is the firſt virtue: it approves acknowledgment, and yet preſerves ingratitude.

It would be laudable in me if I could re-eſtabliſh thee upon the throne of thy fathers: but I am criminal in preſerving for thee ſomething more precious than the empires of the world.

They would commend me if I could recompenſe thy benefits by the treaſures of *Peru*. Stripped of all, dependant for all, I poſſeſs only my love; that they would have me tear from thee, and become ungrateful, becauſe I have virtue. Ah my dear *Aza!* I ſhould deceive them, if I promiſed a moment to ceaſe loving thee. Faithful to their laws, I ſhall be ſo to my love alſo; I ſhall live for thee alone.

LETTER XXIII.

I Believe, my dear *Aza*, that nothing but the joy of ſeeing thee can ſurpaſs that which I felt upon the return of *Deterville:* but, as if I was never more to taſte pleaſures unmixed, it was very ſoon followed by a ſorrow which ſtill endures.

Celina was yeſterday morning in my chamber, when ſomebody came and whiſpered her out, and ſhe had not been long gone, before I was bid to come to the parlour. I ran thither; and how was I ſurprized to find her brother there with her.

I did not diſſemble the pleaſure I received at ſeeing him to whom I owe ſo much eſteem and friendſhip. As ſentiments of this kind border on virtue, I expreſſed them with as much truth as I felt them.

I ſaw

I faw my deliverer, the only fupport of my hope: I began to fpeak without conftraint of thee, of my love, of my defigns, and my joys fwelled up to tranfports.

As I did not fpeak *French* when *Deterville* went away, how many things had I to tell him? how many queftions to afk him, and how many thanks to give him? Defirous to tell him all at once, I fpoke bad *French*, and yet continued to talk on.

During this time I perceived that *Deterville* changed his countenance: the gloom which I remarked on his face when I entered, difappeared: joy took its place; and I, pleafed that I could give him delight, endeavoured to heighten it ftill more. Alas! ought I to have feared giving too much pleafure to a friend to whom I owe all, and from whom I expect all? Yet my fincerity threw him into an error which at prefent cofts me a great many tears.

Celina went out at the fame time that I came in: perhaps her prefence might have hindered fo cruel an explanation.

Deterville, attentive to my words, feemed to take pleafure in hearing them without aiming to interrupt me. I know not what trouble feized me, when I would have demanded of him inftructions relative to my journey, and explained to him the motive of it: but I wanted expreffions, and fearched them in vain. He availed himfelf of a moment of filence, and bowing one knee to the ground before the grate, which he held with both his hands, he faid to me in a paffionate tone; To what fentiments, divine *Zilia*, muft I afcribe the pleafure which I fee fo artlefsly expreffed in your fair eyes, as well as in your difcourfe? Am I the happieft of men, at the very inftant when my fifter defcribed me as the greateft object of compaffion? I know not, anfwered I, what uneafinefs *Celina* can have given you, but I am very fure you fhall never receive any from me. She has told me, replied he, that I ought not to hope for your love.

Mine! cried I, interrupting him, could fhe fay that you have not my love? Ah! *Deterville*, how could your fifter blacken me with fuch a crime? I abhor ingratitude, and fhould hate myfelf if I thought I could ever ceafe loving you.

Whilft I fpoke thefe few words, he feemed by the eagernefs of his looks, as if he would have read my very foul.

You love me then, *Zilia*, faid he, and you tell it me yourfelf! I would have given my life to have heard fo charming a confeffion: but alas! now I hear it, I cannot believe. *Zilia*, my dear *Zilia*, is it true that you love me? Do you not deceive yourfelf; Your tone, your eyes, my heart, every thing feduces me. Perhaps I am only to be plunged again into the defpair from which I have juft efcaped.

You aftonifh me, replied I. Whence arifes your diffidence? Since I have known you, if I could not make myfelf underftood by words, ought not all my actions to have proved that I loved you? No, refumed he, I cannot yet flatter myfelf of this: you are not yet miftrefs enough of *French* to deftroy my juft fears. I know you do not endeavour to deceive me : but tell me what fenfe you affix to thefe adorable words, *I love you.* Let my lot be decided; let me die at your feet, either with grief or pleafure.

Thefe words, I faid to him (a little intimidated by the vivacity with which he concluded his fpeech) thefe words, I think, ought to let you know that you are dear to me ; that I intereft myfelf in your fortune ; that friendfhip and gratitude attach me

to

to you: thefe fentiments pleafe my heart, and ought to fatisfy yours.

Ah *Zilia!* anfwered he, how your expreffions grow more feeble, and your tone more cold! Did *Celina* then tell me truth? Is it not for *Aza* that you feel all that you fay? No, faid I; the fentiments I have for *Aza* are quite different from thofe I have for you: they are what you call *love* in another fenfe. What pain can this give you? added I (feeing him grow pale, leave the grate, and look forrowfully up to heaven) I have this tender love for *Aza*, becaufe he has the fame for me, and we were to be united. There is nothing in this that at all concerns you. There fhould be the fame ties, faid he, betwixt you and me, as you own betwixt him and you, fince I have a thoufand times more love than he ever felt.

How can that be? faid I interrupting. You are not of my nation. Far from having chofen me for your wife, it was chance only that brought us together, and we could never till this day freely communicate our ideas to each other. What reafon could you have to entertain for me fuch fentiments as you mention.

Was any other reafon wanting, he replied, than your charms, and your character, to attach me to you till death? Tenderly educated, indolent, an enemy to artifice, the pains it muft have coft me to engage the hearts of women, and the dread of not finding there that franknefs I defired, gave me only a vague and tranfient relifh for the fex. I lived without paffion till the moment I faw you, when your beauty ftruck me: but its impreffion, perhaps, had been as light as that of many others, if the fweetnefs and fimplicity of your character had not made you appear to me the very object which my imagination had fo often formed.

formed. You know, *Zilia*, whether I have shewn respect to this object of my adoration. What has it cost me to resist the seducing occasions which the familiarity of a long voyage offered me? How many times must your innocence have surrendered to my transports, if I had listened to them? But, far from offending you, I carried my discretion even to silence: I even required my sister not to say a word to you of my love, willing to owe nothing but to yourself alone. Ah, *Zilia*, if so tender a respect does not move you, I will fly: but I perceive that my death will be the price of the sacrifice.

Your death! cried I (affected at the sincere grief which I saw press him down) fatal sacrifice indeed! I know not whether the apprehension of my own would be more frightful to me.

Well then, *Zilia*, said he, if my life is dear to you, order me to live. What must I do, said I. Love me, answered he, as you love *Aza*. I love him always the same, replied I, and shall love him till death. I added, Whether your laws permit you to love two objects in the same manner, I know not; but our customs and my heart forbid it. Be content with the sentiments I promise you; I can have no other. Truth is dear to me, and I tell it to you without disguise.

How you assassinate in cold blood! cried he. Ah, *Zilia!* how do I love you, since I adore even your cruel frankness. Well, continued he (after some moments silence) my love shall surpass your cruelty. Your happiness is dearer to me than my own. Speak to me unreservedly with all this torturing sincerity: what hopes have you with regard to the love you still cherish for *Aza?*

Alas! said I, my hopes are in you only. I then told him, I had learned that a communica-

tion

tion with the Indies was not a thing impoffible: that I flattered myfelf he would procure me the means of returning thither; or at leaft, that he would have the goodnefs to get my knots convey-ed to thee, which would inform thee of my con-dition, and procure me an anfwer to them, that I might know thy deftiny alfo, and conduct myfelf accordingly.

I am going, faid he (with an affected coldnefs) to take the neceffary meafures for difcovering the fate of your lover: you fhall be fatisfied on that head: but in vain do you flatter yourfelf with feeing the happy *Aza* again, who is feparated from you by invincible obftacles.

Thefe words, my dear *Aza,* were a mortal wound to my heart : my tears flowed in abundance, and long hindered me from anfwering *Deterville,* who kept on his fide a melancholy filence. If it be fo, faid I at laft, that I fhall fee him no more, yet will I not live for him the lefs. If your friend-fhip be generous enough to procure us fome cor-refpondence, that fatisfaction fhall fuffice to ren-der my life lefs infupportable ; and I fhall die content, provided you promife to inform him that I loved him dying.

Oh ! this is too much, cried he, rifing up brifk-ly. Yes, if it is poffible, I will be the only one unhappy. You fhall know this heart which you difdain : you fhall fee of what efforts a love like mine is capable, and I will force you at leaft to la-ment me. As he fpoke thefe words he fprung a-way, and left me in a condition which I do not yet well comprehend. I continued ftanding, my eyes fixed on the door by which *Deterville* went out, plunged in a confufion of thoughts, which I ftrove in vain to reduce to order. I fhould have continued

nued there longer, if *Celina* had not come into the parlour.

She afked me, fharply, why her brother was gone fo foon, and I did not conceal from her what had paffed betwixt us.

At firft fhe feemed to grieve for what fhe called her brother's misfortune : then turning her forrow into rage, fhe loaded me with the hardeft reproaches, to which I dared not anfwer a fingle word. What could I have faid to her ? My trou- ·ble did not leave me the liberty of thinking. I went out, and fhe did not follow me. Retiring into my chamber, I ftaid there a whole day with- out daring to appear, without fpeaking to any per- fon, and in fuch a diforder of mind that did not permit me even to write to thee.

Celina's wrath, her brother's defpair, and his laft words, to which I dared not give a favourable fenfe, alternately tormented my foul, and gave me the moft cruel uneafinefs.

At laft I thought, that the, only way to foften my inquietudes, was to paint them to thee, and to fearch in thy love for thofe counfels which I have fo much need of. This error fupported me whilft I was writing : but how fhort a time did it laft ? My letter is written, and the charaɛters are drawn for myfelf only.

Thou art ignorant of what I fuffer, thou doft not even know whether I exift, whether I continue to love thee. *Aza*, my dear *Aza*, thou wilt never know thefe things.

L E T T E R XXIV.

I May juftly call that time an abfence, my dear *Aza*, which is elapfed fince the laft time I wrote to thee.

Some

Some days after the conversation I had with *Deterville*, I fell into a sickness which they call a *fever*. If, as I believe, it was caused by the dolorous passions which then agitated me, I doubt not but it has been lengthened by the sorrowful reflections that have since employed me, and by my regret for having lost the friendship of *Celina*.

Though she seemed to be concerned for my malady, and took of me all the care that was in her power, it was with so cold an air, and so little sympathy in the affliction of my soul, that I cannot doubt but her sentiments towards me are altered. The extreme friendship she has for her brother sets her against me, and she continually reproaches me for having rendered him unhappy. The shame of appearing ungrateful intimidates me : the affected kindnesses of *Celina* torture me : she is constrained by my perplexity, and the soft and agreeable are banished from our conversation.

In spite of so much contrariety and pain from the brother and sister, I am not unaffected with the events which have changed their destiny.

Madame *Deterville* is dead. This unnatural mother has not belied her character ; she has left her whole fortune to her eldest son. There are hopes that the lawyers may hinder the effects of this injustice. *Deterville*, disinterested with regard to himself, takes infinite pains to redeem *Celina* from oppression. Her misfortune seems to redouble his friendship for her : besides that he comes to see her every day, he writes to her night and morning: his letters are full of tender complaints against me, and such lively solicitude for my health, that, though *Celina* affects, in reading them to me, to inform me only of the progress of their affairs, I can easily discover the motive of this pretence.

I do

I do not doubt but *Deterville* writes them on purpofe that they may be read to me: and yet I am perfuaded he would not do it, if he knew the heavy reproaches that always follow thefe lectures. They make their impreffion upon my heart, and forrow confumes me.

Hitherto, in the midft of ftorms, I have enjoyed the weak fatisfaction of living in peace with myfelf. Not a fpot fullied the purity of my foul, nor a remorfe troubled it. But now I cannot think, without a fort of contempt for myfelf, that I fhould make two perfons unhappy to whom I owe my life. How do I interrupt the repofe which but for me they would enjoy! and yet, though I do them all the harm in my power, I am not, nor will I ceafe to be in this refpect criminal. My tendernefs for thee triumphs over my remorfe. *Aza*, how do I love thee!

LETTER XXV.

HOW hurtful, my dear *Aza*, may prudence fometimes be! I have a long time refifted the powerful inftances which *Deterville* had caufed to be made to me, that I would grant him a moment's converfation. Alas! I fhunned my own happinefs. At length, lefs through complaifance than becaufe I was weary of *Celina*'s importunity, I fuffered myfelf to be led to the parlour. At fight of the frightful change in *Deterville*, which makes him fcarce to be known, I ftood confounded, repented already the ftep I had taken, and waited trembling, for the reproaches which I thought he had a right to lay on me. How could I divine that he was going to fill my foul with pleafure?

Pardon me, *Zilia*, faid he, the violence I put on you. I fhould not have obliged you to fee me,

if

if I had not brought you as much joy as you inflict torment on me. Is a moment's fight of you too much to require, in recompence for the cruel facrifice I am going to make you? Then, without giving me time to anfwer, Here, fays he, is a letter from that relation you was fpeaking of. This will inform you of *Aza*'s fituation, and in fo doing, prove, better than all my oaths, how great is the excefs of my love. He then read the letter through. Oh! my dear *Aza*, could I hear it, and not die for joy? It informed me that thy days are preferved, that thou art free, that thou liveft out of danger at the court of *Spain*. What an unhoped for happinefs!

This admirable letter was writ by a man who knows thee, who fees thee, who converfes with thee. Perhaps thy looks were fixed a moment upon this precious paper. I could not take mine from off it. It was with pain I fuppreffed the joyous exclamations that were ready to efcape, and tears of love overflowed my countenance.

If I had followed the motions of my heart, a hundred times fhould I have interrupted *Deterville*, to tell him all that my gratitude infpired : but I did not forget that my felicity would augment his pain, and fo concealed my tranfports, that only my tears were vifible.

You fee, *Zilia*, faid he, after he had done reading, that I have kept my word : you are informed of *Aza*'s fituation : What is there more to be done ? Give your orders without referve ; there is nothing that you have not right to exact of my love, provided it contributes to your felicity.

Though I might have expected this excefs of goodnefs, it neverthelefs furprized and affected me.

I was fome moments perplexed for an anfwer, fearing to aggravate the grief of fo generous a

E   man.

 the

man. I fought for terms that might exprefs the truth of my heart, without offending the fenfibility of his: I could not find them, and yet was obliged to fpeak.

My happinefs, faid I, will never be without mixture, fince I cannot reconcile the duties of love with thofe of friendfhip. I would regain the friendfhip both of you and *Celina*; would never leave you; would for ever admire your virtues, and through my whole life pay the tribute of gratitude which I owe for your goodnefs. I know, that, in removing to a diftance from two perfons fo dear, I fhall carry with me eternal regret. But—

How, *Zilia*, cried he, would you leave us then? Alas! I was not prepared for this fatal refolution, and want courage to fupport it. I had ftrength enough to fee you here in the arms of my rival: the efforts of my reafon, and the delicacy of my love, had confirmed me to bear that mortal blow which I had contrived for myfelf; but I cannot be feparated from you, I cannot renounce the fight of you. No, you fhall not depart, continued he with warmth: do not think of it: you abufe my tendernefs, and tear, without pity, a heart diftracted with love. *Zilia*! cruel *Zilia*! fee my defpair: it is your work. Alas! what return do you make for the moft pure love!

It is you, anfwered I (frightened at his refolution) it is you that aught to be blamed. You blaft my very foul by forcing it to be ungrateful; you lay wafte my heart by a fruitlefs fenfibility! In the name of friendfhip, do not tarnifh a generofity without example, by a defpair which would caufe the bitternefs of my life, and not render you happy. Do not condemn in me the fame fentiment which you cannot furmount, and force me to complain of you unwillingly. Let me cherifh

your

your name, bear it to the utmoſt limits of the world, and make it revered by people who are the adorers of virtue.

I know not how I pronounced theſe words ; but *Deterville*, fixing his eyes upon me, and yet not ſeeming to look, but ſhut up, as it were, in him-ſelf, continued a long time in profound medita-tion. I did not dare to interrupt him, and we kept an equal ſilence till he reſumed his ſpeech, and with a ſort of tranquillity ſaid to me : Yes, *Zilia*, I know, I feel my own injuſtice : but can one coolly renounce the ſight of ſo many charms ? You will have it ſo, and you ſhall be obeyed. O heaven ! what a ſacrifice ! My ſorrowful days ſhall roll on, and end without ſeeing you. At leaſt if death—Let us talk no more of it, added he, in-terrupting himſelf : my weakneſs betrayed me : give me two days to confirm myſelf, and I will wait upon you again, that we may together take the meaſures neceſſary for your journey. Adieu, *Zilia*. May the happy *Aza* taſte all felicity. At ſaying theſe words he went out.

I confeſs to thee, my dear *Aza*, though *Deter-ville* is dear to me, though I was deeply affected with his grief, I had too much impatience to en-joy my felicity in peace not to be very well pleaſ-ed with his retirement.

How delightful is it, after ſo much pain, to give one's ſelf up to joy ! I paſſed the reſt of the day in the moſt tender raptures. I did not write to thee : a letter would have been too little for my heart, it would have recalled thy abſence to my mind. I ſaw thee, I ſpoke to thee, dear *Aza!* What had been wanting to my happineſs, if thou hadſt joined to that precious letter ſome tokens of thy tenderneſs ? Why didſt thou not do it ? They ſpoke to thee concerning me ; thou knoweſt my

ſituation,

fituation, and I heard not a word of thy love. But can I doubt of thy heart? Mine is anfwerable for it. Thou loveft me; thy joy is equal to mine: thou burneft with the fame fire, and the fame impatience devours thee. Let fear be far from my foul, and joy reign there without mixture. Yet —thou haft embraced the religion of that favage people. What is that religion? Does it require the fame facrifices of affection as that of *France?* No: thou wouldft not then have fubmitted to it.

However that be, my heart is under thy laws: fubmitted to thy underftanding, I will blindly adopt whatever may render us infeparable. How can I fear? Soon re-united to my blifs, to my being, to my all, I fhall hereafter think for thee only, and live for nothing but to love thee.

LETTER XXVI.

IT is here, my dear *Aza*, that I fhall fee thee again: my felicity encreafes every day by its particular circumftances. The interview affigned me by *Deterville* is juft over, and whatever pleafure I promifed myfelf in furmounting the difficulties of a long journey, of preventing thee, of meeting thy footfteps, I facrifice it without regret to the happinefs of feeing thee fooner.

Deterville has proved to me, with fuch ftrong evidence, that thou mayeft be here in lefs time than I can travel into *Spain*, that, though he generoufly left to me the choice, I did not hefitate to wait for thee here; time being too precious to be wafted without neceffity.

Perhaps I fhould have examined this advantage with more care, if, before I had chofen, I had not gained fuch lights with refpect to my journey as determined me in secret what party to take, and that secret I can trust only to thee.

I remember that, in the long route which brought me to *Paris*, *Deterville* gave pieces of silver, and sometimes of gold, at all the places where we stopped. I desired to know if this was required of him, or if he did it of mere generosity : and was informed, that, in *France*, travellers pay not only for their food, but even for their repose *. Alas! I have not the least portion of that which would be necessary to satisfy the cravings of this greedy people : all must come from *Deterville*. Thou knowest what I owe him, and how shameful would it be to contract fresh obligations! I should accept his favour with a repugnance, which nothing but absolute necessity could vanquish. Can I voluntarily make myself a greater debtor to him who has already done and suffered so much for me ? I could not resolve on it, my dear *Aza*, and this reason alone would have determined me to remain here. The pleasure of seeing thee sooner only confirmed my former resolution.

Deterville has writ in my presence to the *Spanish* minister : he presses him to let thee come, and points out to him the means of getting thee conducted hither, with a generosity that warms at once my gratitude and admiration.

How pleasant were the moments that passed while *Deterville* was writing ! how delightful to plan out the dispositions for thy journey, to settle the preparations for my happiness, of which I can no longer doubt !

If at first it cost me dear to renounce the design of preventing thy journey, I confess, my dear

E 3 *Aza,*

---

* The *Incas* established large houses upon the road, where all travellers were entertained without expence.

Aza, I have found in fo doing the fource of a thoufand pleafures, which I had not before perceived.

Many circumftances, which at firft appeared not confiderable enough either to haften or retard my journey, become to me interefting and agreeable. I followed blindly the bias of my heart ; and forget that I was coming in fearch of thee among thofe cruel *Spaniards*, the very idea of whom ftrikes me with horror. The certainty of not feeing them any more gives me infinite fatisfaction. Though the voice of love at firft fuppreffed that of friendfhip, I now tafte without remorfe the fweetnefs of uniting them. *Deterville* has affured me, that it will be impoffible for us ever to vifit the city of the fun : and, after our own country, can there be a more agreeable place of refidence than this of *France ?* It will pleafe thee, my dear *Aza*, though fincerity is banifhed from it. Here are fo many agreeable things, that they make one forget the dangers of the fociety.

After what I have faid to thee of gold, it is unneceffary to caution thee to take fome of it with thee : thou wilt have no other merit. A fmall part of thy treafures would amaze and confound the pride of the magnificent indigents of this kingdom : thy virtues and thy fentiments will be cherifhed by me only.

Deterville has promifed to tranfmit to thee my knots, and my letters, and affured me that thou wilt find interpreters to explain the latter. They are come to demand my packet, and I muft have done. Farewell, dear hope of my life : I will continue to write to thee, and, if I cannot fend my letters, will keep them for thee.

How

How should I support the length of thy journey, if I were to deprive myself of the only means I have of conversing with my joy, my transports, my felicity?

LETTER XXVII.

SINCE I know my letters to be upon the road, my dear *Aza*, I enjoy a tranquillity to which I was before a stranger. I think for ever of the pleasure thou wilt have in receiving them; I see and partake thy transports; my soul admits only agreeable ideas, and, to complete my joy, peace is again established in our little society.

The judges have restored to *Celina* the effects of which her mother had deprived her: she sees her lover every day, and her marriage is retarded only by the necessary preparations that are making for it. Thus happy to her wishes, she thinks no more of quarreling with me; and I have as much obligation to her, as if the kindnesses she begins again to shew me were owing to her friendship. Whatever the motive be, we are always in debt to those who help us to the enjoyment of agreeable sentiments.

This morning she made me fully sensible of it by an act of complaisance which at once transported me from tiresome anxiety to the most calm tranquillity.

They had bought her a prodigious quantity of stuffs, garments, and toys of all kinds. She ran and fetched me into the chamber, and, after having consulted me upon the different beauties of so many ornaments, she put together a heap of those which had most attracted my attention, and hastily commanded our *Chinas* to carry them into my apartment, though I opposed it with all my power.

E 4

My

My refusal at firſt diverted her only; but perceiving that the more I declined the preſent, the more ſhe perſiſted in making it, I could no longer diſſemble my reſentment.

Why, ſaid I to her (with my eyes full of tears) why will you humble me more than I am? I owe to you my life, and all that I have: but ſo much bounty is not neceſſary to keep my misfortunes in remembrance. I know that, according to your laws, when benefits are of no advantage to thoſe who receive them, the ſhame is effaced. It is not without repugnance, added I (in a more moderate tone) that I conform to ſentiments which have ſo little of nature in them. Our cuſtoms are more humane: he that receives is honoured as much as he that gives. You have taught me to think otherwiſe; and is not this, therefore, to offer me an outrage?

This amiable friend, melted by my tears more than irritated by my reproaches, anſwered in the moſt kind and gentle tone: Both my brother and I, my dear *Zilia*, would be far from offending your delicacy. It would ill become us as you ſhall know preſently, to affect magnificence in our behaviour to you. I only deſired that you would partake with me the preſents of a generous brother; and I knew this was the moſt certain method of ſhewing him my gratitude. Cuſtom, in my ſituation, authoriſes me to offer you theſe things: but, ſince you are offended, I will ſay no more to you upon the ſubject. You promiſe me then? ſaid I. Yes, anſwered ſhe with a ſmile; but give me leave to write a word or two to *Deterville*.

I let her do as ſhe deſired, and freedom was reſtored betwixt us. We began to examine her dreſs more particularly, till ſhe was called into
the

the parlour. She would have had me go with her: but, my dear *Aza*, can I have any amusement comparable to that of writing to thee? Far from feeking any other, I am apprehenfive before hand of the diverfions intended for me.

Celina is going to be married, and fhe talks of taking me with her: fhe would have me quit this religious houfe, and live in hers. But, if I may be believed - *Aza*, my dear *Aza*, by what an agreeable furprize was my letter interrupted! I believed I had for ever loft this precious monument of our antient fplendor; I had even left off thinking of it: but now I am furrounded with the magnificence of *Peru*; I fee it, I feel it, and fcarce can I believe my eyes or my hands.

Whilft I was writing to thee, *Celina* came into my chamber, followed by four men crouching under the weight of heavy chefts which they had on their backs. They fet them down and retired, and I imagined they had brought fome new prefents from *Deterville*. I already murmured to myfelf, when *Celina*, giving me fome keys, faid, Open, *Zilia*, open without being angry: it comes from *Aza*.

Truth, which I fix infeparably to the idea of thee, did not leave me in the leaft doubt. I opened haftily, and my furprize confirmed my error, when I faw that all which I beheld were the ornaments of the temple of the Sun.

A confufion of thoughts, mixed up of forrow and joy, of pleafure and regret, filled all my heart. I threw myfelf proftrate before thefe facred remains of our worfhip and our altars, covered them with refpectful kiffes, watered them with my tears, and could not be difengaged from

E 5   them:

them: I even forgot that *Celina* was prefent, till fhe roufed me from my trance by giving me a letter, which fhe defired me to read.

Still given up to my error, I thought it came from thee, and my tranfports redoubled: but, though I made it out with pain, I foon perceived that it was *Deterville*'s writing. It will be eafier for me to copy it, my dear *Aza*, than to explain to thee the fenfe of it.

D E T E R V I L L E's B I L L E T.

" Thefe treafures are yours, fair *Zilia*, fince I
" found them in the fhip that carried you. Some
" difputes that arofe among the crew, hindered
" me from difpofing of them freely till now. I
" would have prefented them to you myfelf; but
" the uneafinefs you difcovered to my fifter this
" morning would not permit me to follow my
" inclination. I could not too foon diffipate your
" fears, and I will all my life long prefer your fa-
" tisfaction to mine."

I confefs with a blufh, my dear *Aza*, that I was at that inftant lefs fenfible of *Deterville*'s generofity then of my own pleafure that I was able to give him proofs of mine.

Immediately I fet apart a vafe, which chance, rather than avarice, had caufed to fall into the hands of the *Spainards*. It was the fame (my heart knew it) which thy lips touched on that day when it was thy pleafure to tafte fome *Aca* ✱ prepared by my hand. Richer in this treafure than in all the reft that was reftored to me, I called the men who brought the chefts, and would have had
them

✱ A drink of the Indians.

them take the whole back again as a prefent to *De-terville:* but *Celina* oppofed my defign.

How unjuft you are, *Zilia!* faid fhe. What, would you, who were offended at the offer of a trifle, defire my brother to accept of immenfe riches? Obferve equity in your own actions, if you would infpire others with it.

Thefe words ftruck me, and I perceived there was more of pride and vengeance than of generofity in my action. How near do the vices and virtues approach each other! I confeffed my fault, and afked *Celina*'s pardon: but what afflicted me the moft was, the conftraint fhe laid me under, not to endeavour to repair what I had done. Do not punifh me, faid I, with a timid air, as much as I deferve: difdain not to accept of a few fpecimens of the workmanfhip of our unfortunate countries: you have no need of them, and my requeft ought not to give you offence.

While I fpoke, I obferved that *Celina* looked attentively at fome golden fhrubs, with birds and infects on them of excellent workmanfhip: I inftantly made her a prefent of them, together with a fmall filver bafket, which I filled with flowers and fhells moft curioufly imitated. She accepted it with a goodnefs that tranfported me.

I afterwards chofe out feveral idols of the nations * conquered by thy anceftors, and a fmall ftatue † reprefenting a virgin of the Sun: to thefe I added a tyger, a lion, and other courageous animals,

---

* The *Incas* caufed the idols of the people they fubdued to be depofited in the temple of the Sun, after they had conformed to the worfhip of that luminary. They had idols alfo themfelves, the *Inca Huayna* having confulted that of *Rimace.* See the hiftory of the *Incas.*

† The *Incas* adorned their houfes with ftatues of gold of all magnitudes, even to gigantic fizes.

animals, and befought her to fend them to *Deter-ville*. Write to him then, faid fhe with a fmile : without a letter from you, the prefents will not be well received.

I was too well fatisfied to refufe any thing ; and wrote all that my gratitude dictated : and when *Celina* was gone out, I diftributed fmall prefents to her *China* and mine, and put others afide for my writing-mafter. Then it was that I enjoyed the delicious pleafure of being able to give.

I did not do this without choice, my dear *Aza*. All that came from thee, whatever thou wilt particularly remember, has not gone out of my hands.

The golden chair *, which was kept in the temple for the vifiting days of the *Capa-Inca*, thy auguft father, placed in a corner of my apartment, in form of a throne, reprefents to me thy grandeur, and the majefty of thy rank. The great figure of the Sun, which I myfelf faw torn from the temple by the perfidious *Spaniards*, fufpended over it, excites my veneration. I fall down before it, and adore it in mind, while my heart belongs all to thee.

The two palm-trees, which thou gaveft to the Sun as an offering, and a pledge of the faith thou hadft fworn to me, placed on the two fides of the throne, continually revive in my mind thy tender and affectionate oaths.

Flowers, birds †, difpofed with fymmetry in all the corners of my apartment, form in miniature the image of thofe magnificent gardens, where

* The *Incas* never fat but upon feats of maffy gold.
† The gardens of the temple, and thofe of the royal palaces, were filled with various kinds of imitations in gold and filver. The *Peruvians* made images even of the plant *Mays*, with which they would fill whole fields.

where I have fo often entertained myfelf with thy idea.

My fatisfied eyes can fix in no part without calling to mind thy love, my joy, my blifs, in a word, all that will ever conftitute the life of my life.

LETTER XXVIII.

IT was in vain, my dear *Aza*, that I endeavoured by prayers, complaints, and remonftrances, to avoid quitting my retreat: I have been obliged to give way to *Celina*'s importunities, and we have been now three days in the country, where her marriage was celebrated at our firft arrival.

What pain, what regret, what grief did I not feel at abandoning the dear and precious ornaments of my folitude! Alas! fcarce had I had time to enjoy them, and I fee nothing here to make amends for what I have loft!

The joys and pleafures with which every one here feems intoxicated, are fo far from diverting and amufing me, that they make me remember with greater regret the peaceable days I fpent in writing to, or at leaft in thinking of, thee.

The diverfions of this country appear to me as affected and unnatural as the manners: they confift of a violent gaiety, exprefs'd by loud laughter, in which the foul feems to take no part; of infipid games, in which money makes all the pleafure; or elfe in converfations fo frivolous, in which the fame things are continually repeated, that they refemble rather the chattering of birds than the difcourfe of thinking beings.

The young men, who are here in great number, were at firft very bufy in following and feeming to oblige me: but whether the coldnefs of my converfation has difgufted them, or that my little relifh for their entertainments has made them weary of taking pains to recommend their fervices, two days only were fufficient to make them forget me, and deliver me from their importunate notice.

The propenfity of the *French* is fo natural to extremes, that *Deterville*, though exempt from a great part of the faults of his nation, does yet participate of this.

Not content with keeping the promife he has made, of not fpeaking his fentiments any more to me, he with remarkable caution avoids ftaying where I am prefent : fo that though we are obliged to fee one another continually, I have not yet found an opportunity of talking with him.

By the forrow that opprefles him amidft the public joy, I can eafily perceive that in this fhynefs he commits a violence on himfelf. Perhaps I ought to be obliged to him for it : but I have fo many queftions to afk him about thy departure from *Spain*, thy arrival here, and other fuch interefting fubjects, that I cannot pardon while I am forced to approve his conduct. I defire violently to oblige him to fpeak to me; but the dread of reviving his complaints and regrets prevents my doing it.

Celina, intirely taken up with her new fpoufe, affords me no relief, and the reft of the company are not agreeable to me. Thus, alone in the midft of a tumultuous affembly, I have no amufement but my thoughts, which are all addreffed to thee. My dear *Aza*, thou fhalt ever be the fole confident of my heart, my pleafures, my felicity.

END of VOLUME FIRST.

LETTERS

WRITTEN BY A

PERUVIAN PRINCESS.

A NEW EDITION.

IN TWO VOLUMES.

VOL. II.

DUBLIN:

Printed for WILLIAM COLLES, in Dame-ſtreet;
and RICH. MONCRIEFFE, in Capel-ſtreet.

M.DCC.LXXIV.

LETTERS

PERUVIAN LADY.

LETTER XXIX.

I Was much to blame, my dear *Aza*, in defiring fo earneftly a converfation with *Deterville*. He hath faid but too much to me : though I difallow the trouble that he has excited in my foul, it is not yet effaced.

I know not what fort of impatience was added yefterday to my ufual melancholy : the world, and the noife of it, became to me more troublefome than ordinary. Except the tender fatisfaction of *Celina* and her hufband, every thing that I faw infpired me with an indignation bordering on contempt. Afhamed to find fuch unjuft fentiments in my heart, I endeavoured to hide the perplexity they caufed me in the moft retired part of the garden.

Scarce had I fat me down at the foot of a tree, before the tears involuntarily flowed down my cheeks. With my face hid betwixt my hands, I

was

was buried in fo profound a reverie, that *Deter-ville* was on his knees by the fide of me before I perceived him.

Be not offended, *Zilia*, faid he: it is chance that has brought me to your feet, I was not look-ing after you. Weary of the tumult, I was co-ming to enjoy my forrow in peace. I perceived you, and ftruggled with myfelf to keep at a dif-tance from you: but I am too unhappy to conti-nue fo without feeking relief. In pity to myfelf I drew near; I faw your tears flow, and was no longer mafter of my powers.—But, if you com-mand me to fly from you, I will obey. Can you do it, *Zilia?* Am I odious to you?—No, faid I: on the contrary, fit down, I am glad to have an opportunity of fpeaking to you fince the laft benefits your conferred on me.—Let us not talk of them, interrupted he brifkly.—But hear me, replied I: to be entirely generous, you muft liften to acknow-ledgment. I have not fpoken to you fince you re-ftored to me the precious ornaments of the temple in which I was educated. Perhaps in my letter I badly expreffed the fentiments that fuch an excefs of goodnefs infpired me with: but I meant———— Alas! interrupted he again, what comfort does ac-knowledgment bring to a heart that is wretched? Thanks are the companions of indifference, and too often allied with hatred.

What is that you fay? cried I. Why do you thus wrong me in your thoughts? Ah! *Deterville*, what a right fhould I have to reproach you, if you were not fo much to be pitied! Far from hating you, ever fince the firft moment I faw you, I have depended on you with lefs repugnance than on the *Spaniards.* Your gentlenefs and kindnefs have made me all along defire to gain your friendfhip, in proportion as I faw farther into your character.

I am

I am confirmed in the opinion that you deferve all
mine; and, without fpeaking of the extreme obligations I have to you (fince my acknowledgment
difpleafes) how could I help entertaining the fentiments which are fo juftly your due?

Your virtues alone I found worthy of the fimplicity of ours: a fon of the Sun would be honoured by
your fentiments: your reafon is like that of nature:
How many motives then had I to efteem you? Even
the noblenefs of your figure, and every thing about
you, pleafes me: for friendfhip has eyes as well as
love. Heretofore, after a fhort abfence, you never came to me again but I felt a fort of ferenity
expand in my heart. Why have you changed thofe
innocent pleafures into pains and anxieties?

Your reafon now appears but in ftarts only,
and I am continually afraid of thofe fallies. The
fentiments you entertain me with lay a reftraint on
the expreffion of mine, and deprive me of the pleafure of defcribing to you, without difguife, the
charms I could tafte in your friendfhip, if you did
not yourfelf difturb the fweetnefs of it. You even
take from me the delicate pleafure of looking on
my benefactor: your eyes perplex mine, and I
no more obferve in them that agreeable tranquillity
which hath fometimes paffed to my very foul. Your
conftant and fettled melancholy reproaches me
eternally with being the caufe of it. Ah *Deterville!* how unjuft are you, if you think you fuffer alone.

My dear *Zilia*, cried he (kiffing my hand with
ardour) what an addition does your kindnefs and
franknefs of fpeech make to my regret! What a
treafure would the poffeffion of fuch a heart as
yours be! But with what aggravated defpair do
you make me fenfible of the lofs of it!

Mighty

Mighty *Zilia*, continued he, how great is your power? Was it not enough to convert me from the moſt careleſs indifference to love, from indolence to fury, but you muſt vanquiſh me too? Can I bear it?—Yes, ſaid I; this effort is worthy of your noble heart: an action ſo juſt and generous elevates you above mortals.—But can I ſurvive it? reſumed he ſorrowfully. Do not hope, however, that I ſhall ſerve for the victim of your love: I will continue ſtill to adore your idea, which ſhall be the bitter nouriſhment of my ſoul. I will love you, and ſee you no more. Oh!—But at leaſt do not forget.—

The riſing ſobs choaked his ſpeech, and he haſtily endeavoured to hide the tears which overflowed his face. Affected equally with his generoſity and his grief, I ſhed ſome myſelf, and preſſed one of his hands in mine. No, ſaid I, you ſhall not leave me. Let me ſtill keep my friend, and be you ſatisfied with thoſe ſentiments which I ſhall have for you all my life long. I love you almoſt as much as I love *Aza*, but I cannot love you in the ſame manner as him.

Cruel *Zilia*, cried he with tranſport, will you always accompany your goodneſs with ſuch piercing ſtrokes? Muſt a mortal poiſon continually deſtroy the charm that you convey with your words? How ſenſeleſs am I to be bewitched by their ſweetneſs! to what a ſhameful humility do I degrade myſelf! But it is done, I recover myſelf, added he in a firm tone. Farewell; you ſhall ſoon ſee *Aza*; may he not make you feel torments like thoſe which prey on me; may he be ſuch as your deſire makes him, and worthy of your heart!

You cannot conceive, my dear *Aza*, what an alarm the air he pronounced theſe words in, gave to my ſoul. I could not guard againſt the ſuſpi-
cions

cions that came crowding into my mind. I did not doubt but *Deterville* was better informed than he cared to appear, and had concealed from me some letters that he had received from *Spain:* in short (shall I dare pronounce it?) I suspected that thou wert unfaithful.

I intreated him, in the strongest manner, to tell me the truth: but all that I could get out of him amounted only to loose conjectures, which had an equal tendency to confirm and to destroy my fears.

However, reflections upon the inconstancy of men, the dangers of absence, and the facility with which thou hadst changed thy religion, remained deeply graven upon my mind.

Now did my love, for the first time, become to me a painful sentiment; now was I for the first time, afraid of losing thy heart. *Aza,* if it were true, if thou didst not love me, would that my death had separated us, rather than thy inconstancy!

No; it was his own despair that suggested to *Deterville* these frightful ideas. Ought not his trouble and distraction to convince me of it? Should not his self interest, which makes him speak, be called in question by me? It was so, my dear *Aza,* and my resentment turned all against him. I treated him roughly, and he quitted me in a desperate fury.

Alas! was I less desperate than he? What torments did I not suffer, before I found again the repose of my heart? Is it yet well confirmed? *Aza!* I love thee so tenderly, canst thou forget me?

LETTER

LETTER XXX.

THY journey, my dear *Aza*, feems to me very long. How ardently do I defire thy arrival! Time has diſſipated my inquietudes, and I now eſteem them only as a dream, of which the light of the day has effaced the impreſſion. I accuſe myſelf of a crime in having ſuſpeɛted thee, and my repentance redoubles my tendernefs: it has almoſt rooted out my compaſſion for the pains of *Deterville*. I cannot pardon him for the ill opinion he ſeems to have of thee, and I have lefs regret than ever in being as it were ſeparated from him.

We have been at *Paris* a fortnight, and I live with *Celina* in her huſband's houſe which is ſo diſtant from that of her brother, that I am not obliged to ſee him every hour. He often comes hither to eat: but *Celina* and I live together in ſuch a hurry, that he has not leiſure to ſpeak with me in private.

Since our return, we employ part of the day in the tireſome work of dreſſing ourſelves, and the reſt in what they call here paying of viſits.

Theſe two occupations ſeem to me quite as unprofitable as they are fatiguing, if the latter did not procure me the means of informing myſelf more particularly of the cuſtoms of the country.

At my arrival in *France*, not underſtanding the language, I could judge of things only by their outſide. As I had little inſtruɛtion in the religious houſe, I found the country turned to no better account, where I ſaw only a particular ſociety, with which I was too much tired to examine it. It is here only, that, by converſing with what they call the great world, I ſee the whole nation.

The

The vifits or *devoirs* that we pay, confift in going to as great a number of houfes as poffible, there
to give and receive a reciprocal tribute of praife
upon the beauty of our faces and fhapes, the ex-
cellence of our tafte, and the judicious choice of
our dreffes.

It was not long before I difcovered the reafon
that made us take fo much pains to acquire this
homage: I find it is, becaufe there is a neceffity
of receiving in perfon this momentary incenfe : for
no fooner does any one difappear, but fhe takes
another form. The charms that were found in
her that goes out ferve only to make a contemptuous comparifon, in order to eftablifh the perfections of her who comes in.

Cenfure is the reigning tafte of the *French*, as
incoherence is the character of their nation. In
their books, you find the general criticifm of human manners, and in their converfation that of
every particular perfon, provided he be abfent.

What they call the mode, has not altered the
antient ufage of faying freely all the ill they can
of others, and fometimes even more than they
think. People of the beft behaviour follow the
cuftom, and are diftinguifhed only by a certain
formal apology they make for their franknefs and
love of truth: which once over, they reveal the
faults, the ridicules, and even the vices, of others
without fcruple, not fparing even their beft friends.

As the fincerity which the *French* ufe to one
another is without exception, fo their reciprocal
confidence is without bounds. One need have
neither eloquence to be heard, nor probity to obtain belief. Every thing is faid, every thing is received, with the fame levity.

Yet I would not have you think, my dear *Aza*,
that the *French* are in general born with bad inclinations:

clinations : I fhould be more unjuft than they if
I left you in fuch an error.

Naturally fufceptible of virtuous fentiments, I
never faw one of them that was not melted at the
hiftory, which they oblige me often to give them,
of the rectitude of our hearts, the candour of our
fentiments, and the fimplicity of our manners. If
they lived amongft us, they would become virtuous : but example and cuftom are the tyrants by
which they are fway'd.

A man of good fenfe fpeaks ill of the abfent,
becaufe he would not be defpifed by thofe who are
prefent : another would be honeft, humane, and
without pride, if he did not fear being ridiculous ;
and a third becomes ridiculous thro' fuch qualities,
as would make him a model of perfection if he
dared to exert them, and affume his juft merit.

In a word, my dear *Aza*, their vices are artificial as well as their virtues, and the frivoloufnefs
of their character permits them to be but imperfectly what they are. Like the play-things they
give their children, thefe whimfical people fhew
only a faint refemblance of the thinking beings
they fhould appear. You have weight, foftnefs,
colour, and upon the whole a fair outfide, without
any real value. Accordingly they are efteemed
by other nations only as the pretty toys and trifles
of fociety. Good fenfe fmiles at their genteel airs,
and coldly ranks them in their proper place.

Happy the nation which has nature only for its
guide, truth for its mover, and virtue for its principle.

LETTER

LETTER XXXI.

IT is not furprizing, my dear *Aza*, that inco-herence is a confequence of the airy character of the *French*: but I cannot be enough furprized that they, with as much or more penetration than any other nation, feem not to perceive the fhock-ing contradictions which foreigners remark in them at the firft fight.

Among the great number of thofe which ftrike me every day, I do not fee any one that more dif-honours their underftanding, than their manner of thinking with regard to women. They refpect them, my dear *Aza*, and at the fame defpife them with equal excefs.

The firft law of their politenefs, or virtue (I do not know that they have any other) regards the women. A man of the higheft rank owes the utmoft complaifance to a women of the moft vile condition, and would blufh for fhame, and think himfelf ridiculous in the higheft degree, if he offer-ed her any perfonal infult. And yet a man of the leaft confideration and credit may deceive and be-tray a woman of merit, and blacken her reputation without fear of either blame or punifhment.

If I was not affured that thou wilt foon be a judge of thefe things thyfelf, fcarce fhould I dare paint to thee fuch contrafts as the fimplicity of our minds cannot without pain conceive. Docile to the noti-ons of nature, our genius proceeds no farther: we have found that the ftrength and courage of one fex indicates that it ought to be the fupport and defence of the other, and our laws are conforma-ble to this difcovery *. Here, far from compaffi-

F   onating

* The *Peruvian* laws difpenfe the women from all hard bodily labour.

onating the weaknefs of women, thofe of the common people, tied down to labour, have no relief
either from the laws or their hufbands. Thofe of
more elevated rank, the prey either of the feduction or malice of men, have no recompence for the
perfidies impofed on them, except a fhew of merely imaginary outfide refpeʊt, which is continually
followed by the moft ftinging fatire.

I perfeʊtly well perceived, when I firft converfed
in the world here, that the habitual cenfure of the
nation falls principally upon the women, and that
the men do not defpife one another without fome
caution or referve. I looked for the caufe of this
in their good qualities, when an accident revealed
it to me among their defeʊts.

In all the houfes we have entered for two days
paft, we have been told of the death of a young
man killed by one of his friends, and the barbarous
aʊtion is approved of for no other reafon, but becaufe the dead had fpoken to the difadvantage of
the living. This new extravagance feemed of fo
ferious a charaʊter, as to deferve my exaʊteft en-
quiry. Upon information, my dear *Aza*, I learned that a man is obliged to expofe his life to take
away that of another, if he hears that this other
has been talking againft him; or to banifh himfelf from fociety, if he refufes to take fo cruel a
vengeance. I wanted to be told no more, in order
to form a clear idea of what I fought. It is certain
that the men, naturally cowards, without fhame,
and without remorfe, are afraid only of corporal
punifhments. And if the women were authorifed
to punifh the outrages offered them in the fame
manner, as the men are obliged to revenge the
flighteft infult offered to one another, fuch perfons as we fee now well received in fociety,
would not be fo any longer. The flanderer muft
retire

retire into a defert, and there hide his malice and
his fhame. But cowards have nothing to fear, and
have too well founded this abufe to fee it ever abo-
lifhed.

Impudence and effrontery are the firft fentiments
that the men are infpired with : timidity, gentlenefs, and patience, are the fole virtues that are
cultivated in the women: How then are thefe to
avoid being the victims of impunity ?

O my dear *Aza*, let not the brilliant vices of a
nation, otherwife charming, give us a difguft of
the natural fimplicity of our own manners! Let
us not forget; thou, the obligation thou art under
to be my example, my guide, and my fupport in
the path of virtue ; I, the duty that lies on me to
preferve thy efteem and thy love, by imitating my
model, even by furpaffing it if poffible, and me-
riting a refpect founded on virtue, and not on a
frivolous cuftom.

LETTER XXXII.

OUR vifits and fatigues, my dear *Aza*, could
not end more agreeably. What a delicious
day did I fpend yefterday ! How pleafant are already the new obligations, which *Deterville* and his
fifter confer on me! and how dear will they be
when I can partake them with thee !

After two days reft, we fet out yefterday morning from *Paris*, *Celina*, her brother, her hufband,
and I, to go, as fhe told me, and pay a vifit to the
beft of her friends. The journey was not long,
and we arrived early in the day at a country-houfe,
the fituation and avenues of which appeared to me
admirable: but what aftonifhed me at going in
was, to find all the doors open, and not to meet a
fingle perfon.

This

This houfe, too pretty to be abandoned, too fmall to hide the people which fhould inhabit it, feemed to me a kind of enchantment. I was diverted with the thought, and afked *Celina*, if we were in the dwelling of one of thofe fairies, of whom fhe had made me read the hiftories, where the miftrefs of the manfion and her domeftics were all invifible.

You fhall fee the miftrefs, anfwered fhe; but, as important affairs have called her away for the whole day, fhe has charged me to prevail on you to do the honours of her houfe during her abfence. She added, laughing, Let us fee how you will get off. I came readily into the joke, and put on a ferious air, to copy the compliments which I had heard made on like occafions. They told me I acquitted myfelf pretty well.

After amufing ourfelves for fome time in this manner, *Celina* faid, This politenefs would be fufficient to give us a good reception at *Paris*; but, madam, fomething more muft be done in the country. Will you not have the goodnefs to afk us to dinner?

Upon this head, faid I, I am not knowing enough to give you fatisfaction, and I begin to fear that your friend has relied too much on my care. I know a remedy for that, anfwered *Celina*; if you will only take the pains to write your name, you fhall fee that it is not fo difficult as you think to treat your friends well. You give me comfort, faid I; let me write immediately.

I had no fooner pronounced thefe words, but I faw a man come in dreffed in black, with a ftandifh in his hand, and paper already writ upon. They placed it before me, and I wrote my name where I was directed.

At that inftant another well looking man appeared

peared, who invited us, in the usual manner, to attend him into the dining room.

We there found a table covered with equal propriety and magnificence : scarce were we seated when delightful music was heard in the next room : nothing in short, was wanting that could render a repast agreeable. *Deterville* himself seemed to have forgot his melancholy, in order to make us merry : he expressed his passion to me in a thousand manners, but always in a pleasant tone, without complaints or reproaches.

The day was serene, and, with common consent we agreed to walk when we rose from table. We found the gardens much more extensive than the house seemed to promise : art and symmetry made themselves admired, by uniting to render the charms of simple nature more transporting.

The end of our walk was a wood, which terminates this fine garden: there sitting all four on a delightful turf, we began already to indulge that reverie which natural beauties naturally inspire, when, through the trees, we saw coming on one side a company of peasants, properly dressed in their manner, preceded by some instruments of music, and, on the other side, a company of young lasses, dressed in white, their heads adorned with flowers of the field, who sung in a rustic, but melodious manner, songs, in which, to my surprize, I heard my own name often repeated.

My astonishment was much greater, when the two companies being come up to us, the most distinguished man quitted his, kneeled down on one knee, and presented to me, in a large bason, several keys, with a compliment which my perplexity did not suffer me to understand: I only comprehended in it, that being the chief of the villagers in that country, he came to do me homage in quality

lity of their fovereign, and prefent me with the keys of the houfe of which I was alfo the miftrefs.

As foon as he had ended his. harangue, he rofe to make room for the prettieft of the young dam-fels : fhe prefented me with a bundle of flowers adorned with ribbands, which fhe 'accompanied alfo with a fhort difcourfe in my praife, 'delivered with a good grace.

I was too much confufed, my dear *Aza*, to anfwer eulogies which I fo little deferved ; other-wife, every thing that paffed had an air fo refem-bling that of truth, that many times I could not help believing what neverthelefs I thought incre-dible. This thought produced variety of others, and my mind was fo engaged, that it was impof-fible for me to fpeak a word. If my confufion was diverting to the company, it was not fo to my-felf.

Deterville was the firft who took pity of me: he made a fign to his fifter, who, after having given fome pieces of gold to the lads and laffes, and told them that thofe were the earneft of my kindnefs towards them, arofe, and propofed to take a turn into the wood. I followed her with pleafure, in-tending to have reproached her heartily for the dif-order fhe had put me into: but I had not time; for fcarce had we taken half a dozen fteps before fhe ftopped, and, looking on me with a fmiling coun-tenance, Tell me, *Zilia*, faid fhe, are you not very angry with us? and will you not be more fo if I affure you, that this land and this houfe do in very truth belong to you?

To me? cried I. Ah *Celina*, whether it be an affront or a jeft, you carry it too far. Hear me, faid fhe, more ferioufly: If my brother has difpof-ed of fome parts of your treafure to purchafe it, and, inftead of the difagreeable formalities that
would

would have been otherwife neceffary, referved to
you only the furprize when the thing was done,
ought you to hate us mortally for fo doing? Cannot you pardon us for having procured you, at all
events, fuch a dwelling as you have feemed to like,
and for having fecured to you an independent life?
You, this morning, figned the authentic deed
that puts you in poffeffion of both. Murmur at us
now as much as you pleafe, added fhe, fmiling
again, if nothing of all this be agreeable to you.

Oh my amiable friend! cried I, throwing myfelf at her feet, I have too lively a fenfe of your
generous cares to exprefs my acknowledgment.
Thefe few words were all I was able to utter, my
fecret wifh having before been to have fuch an
independency. Melting in rapturous tranfports,
while I reflected on the pleafure I fhould have in
confecrating to thee this charming abode, the
multitude of my fentiments ftifled the expreffions
of them. I embraced *Celina*, who repayed my
careffes with the fame tendernefs; and, after having given me time to recover myfelf, we returned
to her brother and her hufband.

Trouble feized me again when I came near *Deterville*, and caufed a frefh perplexity in my expreffions. I gave him my hand, which he kiffed
without fpeaking a word, and turned afide to hide
the tears he could not reftrain; which I took for
figns of his fatisfaction on feeing me fo contented.
I was fo moved myfelf as to fhed fome likewife.
Celina's hufband, lefs concerned than we at what
had paffed, foon turned the converfation again
into a pleafant vein: he complimented me on my
new dignities, and prevailed on me to return to
the houfe, in order, as he faid, to examine the defects of it, and fhew *Deterville* that his tafte was
not fo good as he flattered himfef.

F 4

Shall

Shall I confefs to thee, my dear *Aza*, that every thing on our way feemed now to put on a new form ; that the flowers appeared more beautiful, the trees more verdant, and the fymmetry of the garden more complete.

I found more conveniency in the houfe, more richnefs in the furniture, and the fmalleft trifle became now a matter of concern to me.

I ran through the apartments in fuch a rapture of joy, that I did not examine any thing minutely: the only place I ftopped in was a room moderately large, furrounded with cafes curioufly wrought, and covered with gold, in which there were a great number of books of all colours, of all forms, and admirably neat. I was fo enchanted, that I thought I could not have left them till I had read them all; but *Celina* pulled me away, putting me in mind of a golden key which *Deterville* had given me. We endeavoured to make ufe of it ; but our endeavours would have been in vain, if he had not fhewn us the door it was to open ; which was fo artificially concealed in the wainfcot, that it had been impoffible to difcover it without knowing the fecret.

I opened it haftily, and ftood immoveable at the fight of the magnificence it had enclofed.

It was a clofet all brilliant with glafs and painting: the ground of the wainfcot was green, adorned with figures extremely well defigned, and imitating part of the fports and ceremonies of the city of the Sun, in fuch manner as I had related them to *Deterville*.

Virgins were there feen reprefented in a thoufand places, in the fame drefs that I wore when I came into *France:* and I was even told that they were like me.

The

The ornaments of the temple, which I had left in the religious houfe, fupported by gilt pyramids, adorned all the corners of this magnificent cabinet. The figure of the Sun, fufpended in the midft of a cieling painted with the moft beautiful colours of the heavens, completed, by its luftre, the embel-lifhment of this charming folitude; and commo-dious moveables, fuited to the paintings, rendered the whole delicious.

In examining more nearly what I was ravifhed to find again, I perceived that the golden chair was wanting: though I avoided fpeaking of it, *Deterville* guefTed my thoughts, and feized that moment to exprefs himfelf. You fearch in vain, faid he, fair *Zilia:* the chair of the *Incas*, by a ma-gical power, is transformed into a houfe, a garden, and an eftate: if I have not employed my own fcience in this metamorphofis, it was not without regret; but it was necefTary to fhew refpeÊt to your delicacy. See here, added he (opening a little buffet that was dexteroufly funk into the wall) thefe are the remains of the magical operations. At the fame time he fhewed me a ftrong box full of pieces of gold, all of the *French* coin. You know, con-tinued he, that this is not one of the leaft neceffa-ry things among us, and I thought it my duty to preferve you a fmall provifion of it.

I began to exprefs my grateful thanks, and the admiration I was in of fo many preventing cares, when *Celina* interrupted me, and pulled me into a room by the fide of this marvellous clofet. I would, faid fhe, fhew you the power of my art alfo. Large drawers were then opened, full of rich filks, linens, ornaments, in a word, of whatever is worn in the drefs of women, all in fuch abun-dance, that I could not help laughing, and afk-ing *Celina* how many years fhe defired me to

F 5   live,

live, to make ufe of fo many fine things? As long
as I and my brother live, anfwered fhe. And for
my part, replied I, I defire you may both live as
long as I love you, then I am fure you will not die
before me.

As I ended thefe words, we returned, into the
temple of the Sun, which is the name they gave to
that wonderful clofet; and, having at laft freedom of utterance, I exprefled the fentiments of my
heart juft as I felt them. What goodnefs! what a
train of virtues in thefe proceedings of the brother
and fifter!

We fpent the reft of the day in the delights of
confidence and friendfhip. I endeavoured to re-
gale them at fupper ftill more gaily than I had done
at dinner. I gave orders freely to the fervants,
which I knew to be mine; jefted upon my authority and opulence, and did all in my power to render their own benefits agreeable to my benefactors.

I fancied, however, that I perceived, in proportion as time wore away, that *Deterville* fell
again into his melancholy, and even that *Celina* let
drop fome tears between whiles; but they both fo
readily refumed a ferene air, that I again thought
myfelf deceived.

I endeavoured to prevail on them to ftay fome
days, and enjoy with me the good fortune they had
procured. This I could not obtain: we came back
the fame night, promifing ourfelves to return
fpeedily to my enchanted palace.

O my dear *Aza*, how great will be my felicity
when I can inhabit it with thee!

LETTER XXXIII.

THE forrow of *Deterville* and his fifter, my dear *Aza*, has continued to augment fince our return from my enchanted palace. They are both fo dear to me, that I could not forbear being earneft with them to difcover to me the motive of it : but, feeing them obftinately filent upon the fubject, I did not doubt but fome new misfortune had retarded thy journey : and, in a fhort time, my uneafinefs, of which I did not diffemble the caufe, overcame the refolution of my amiable friends.

Deterville confeffed that he had determined to conceal from me the day of thy arrival, in order to furprize me; but that my inquietude made him relinquifh his defign: in fact, fhe fhewed me a letter from the guide which he caufed to be appointed thee, and, by the calculation of the time, and the place where it was wrote, he made me underftand that thou mayft be here to-morrow, to-day or even this very moment; in fhort, that I have no more time to meafure, till the inftant arrives which will crown all my vows.

Having gone thus far, *Deterville* did not hefitate telling me all the reft of his difpofitions: he fhewed me the appartment which he deftined for thee; for thou wilt lodge here, till, united together, decency permits us to inhabit my delicious caftle. I will not lofe fight of thee any more; nothing fhall feparate us: *Deterville* has provided every thing, and convinced me more than ever of the excefs of his generofity.

After he had given me thefe informations, I was no longer to feek for the caufe of that forrow which devours him. It is thy near arrival: I pity him, I
compaffionate

compaffionate his grief, and wifh him an happinefs, independant of my fentiments, which my be a worthy recompence of his virtue.

I diffemble even a part of the tranfports of my joy, that I may not irritate his pain. This is all I can do: but my own felicity engages me too much for me to keep it entirely hidden: therefore, though I believe thee very near me, though my heart leaps at the leaft noife, though I interrupt my letter almoft at every word to run to the window, yet I continue writing to thee: finding this relief to the tranfports of my heart neceffary. Thou art near me, it is true: but is thy abfence lefs real than if we were ftill feparated by the feas? I do not fee thee: thou canft not hear me: why then fhould I ceafe to converfe with thee by the only means in my power? But a moment more, and I fhall fee thee: but this moment does not yet exift. Can I better employ fo much of thy abfence, as I am yet to bear, than by painting to thee the vivacity of my tendernefs? Alas! thou haft hitherto feen it breathing in fighs only! Let that time be far from me! with what tranfport will it be effaced from my memory! *Aza*, dear *Aza!* how fweet is that name to me! Very foon I fhall no longer call thee in vain: thou wilt hear me, and fly to my voice. The moft tender expreffions of my heart fhall be the reward of thy hafte.————I am interrupted: it is not by thee, and yet I muft quit this converfation with thee.

LETTER XXXIV.

To the Chevalier Deterville, *at* MALTA.

WERE you able, Sir, to forefee, without reluctance, the mortal chagrin you were going to join to the happiness you had prepared for me? How could you have the cruelty to caufe your departure to be preceded by fuch agreeable circumftances, by fuch weighty motives of gratitude, unlefs it were to render me more fenfible of your defpair and your abfence? Though but two days ago wrapt up in the fweets of friendfhip, I I now feel the moft bitter anxiety.

Celina, all afflicted as fhe is, has but too well executed your orders. She prefented to me *Aza* with one hand, and your cruel letter with the other. At the completion of my vows grief darted through my foul: while I found the object of my tender love, I did not forget that I loft that of all my other fentiments. Ah *Deterville!* how inhuman this once is your love. But do not hope to execute your unjuft refolution to the utmoft. The fea fhall not make a total feparation betwixt perfons fo dear to each other: my name fhall reach you: you fhall receive my letters, you fhall hear my prayers: blood and friendfhip fhall refume their rights over your heart, and you fhall reftore yourfelf to a family, to which I am refponfible for your lofs.

What! in recompence of fo many benefits, fhall I poifon all your days, and thofe of your fifter? fhall I break fo tender an union? fhall I fix defpair in your hearts, while I ftill enjoy your bounties? No, think not of it. I look on myfelf with horror in a houfe which I fill with mourning: I ac-

knowledge

knowledge your cares in the good treatment I receive from *Celina*, at the very time when I could pardon her for hating me. But whatever thofe cares are, I renounce them all, and remove for ever from a place which I cannot bear, unlefs you return.

Deterville, how very blind you are! What error is it that hurries you away in a defign fo cantrary to your views? You would render me happy, and you only make me culpable: you would dry up my tears, and you caufe them to flow: by your abfence you deftroy all the fruit of your felf-denial.

Alas! you would have found but too much delight in that interview which you dreaded as fo very formidable! This *Aza*, the objeét of fo much love, is no more the fame *Aza* that I have painted to you in fuch tender colours. The coldnefs of his approach, the praifes of the *Spaniards*, with which he a hundred times interrupted the foft overflowings of my foul, the offenfive curiofity which fnatched him from my tranfports to vifit the rarities of *Paris*; all made me in dread of ills at which my heart fhudders. Oh *Deterville*! perhaps you may not be long the moft unhappy.

If compaffion of yourfelf can work nothing on you, let the duties of friendfhip call you back: friendfhip is the only afylum of unfortunate love. If the ills that I dread fhould overwhelm me, what will you not have to reproach yourfelf with? If you abandon me, where fhall I find a heart fenfible of my pains? Shall generofity, hitherto the moft potent of your paffions, give way at laft to difcontented love? No; I cannot believe it: fuch a weaknefs would be unworthy of you: you are incable of delivering yourfelf up to it: but come and convince me, if you love your own glory, and my repofe. L E T-

L E T T E R XXXV.

To the Chevalier Deterville, *at* MALTA.

IF you were not the moſt noble of creatures, Sir,
I ſhould be the moſt abjeƈt. If you had not
the moſt humane of ſouls, the moſt compaſſionate·
of hearts, would it have been to you that I ſhould
have choſen to confeſs my ſhame and my deſpair?
But alas! what remains for me to fear? why ſhould
I pauſe? Every thing to me is loſt.

It is not the loſs of my liberty, of my rank, of
my country, that I now deplore : they are not the
inquietudes of an innocent tenderneſs that now
draw tears from me : it is the violation of good faith;
it is love deſpiſed that rends my ſoul. *Aza* is unfaithful?—*Aza unfaithful*!—What power have
thoſe fatal words over my ſoul!—My blood is frozen—a torrent of tears——

I learned from the *Spaniards* to know misfortunes :
but the laſt is the moſt ſenſible of all their ſtrokes.
It is they that have robbed me of *Aza's* heart; it
is their cruel religion that renders me odious in his
eyes. That religion approves, it ordains infidelity, perfidy, ingratitude : but it forbids the love
of one's near relations. If I were a ſtranger, unknown, *Aza* might love me : but, being united to·
him by the ties of blood, he muſt abandon me, he
muſt take away my life without ſhame, without
regret, without remorſe.

Alas! contradiƈtory as this religion is, if nothing had been neceſſary but to embrace it, in order to recover the good it had deprived me of, I
could have ſubmitted my mind to its illuſions,
without corrupting my heart by its principles. In
the bitterneſs of my ſoul I demanded to be inſtruƈt-
ed

ed in it. My tears were not regarded. I cannot
be admitted into a fociety fo pure, without abandoning the motive which determines me to defire it
—without renouncing my love; that is to fay,
without changing my exiftence.

This extreme feverity, I muft confefs, ftruck
me with awe at the fame time that my heart revolt-
ed againft it: I cannot refufe a fort of veneration
to laws that kill me: But is it in my power to adopt
them? And if I fhould adopt them, what advantage would refult from it? *Aza* loves me not: Oh!
wretch that I am!—

The cruel *Aza* has preferved nothing of the candour of our manners, except that refpect for truth
of which he makes fo cruel an ufage. Seduced by
the charms of a young *Spnniard*, ready to be united with her, he confented to come into *France*
only to difengage himfelf from the faith he had
fworn to me, and to leave me without any doubt
of his real fentiments; only to reftore to me a liberty which I deteft, or, rather, to take away my
life.

Yes, it is in vain that he reftores me to myfelf,
my heart is with him, and will be fo till death.

My life belongs to him: let him take it from me;
—but let him love me.—

. You knew my misfortune: why then did you
only half inform me of it? Why did you give me
room for fufpicions only, which made me unjuft
to you? Alas! why do I impute this to you as a
crime! I fhould not have believed you: blind and
prepoffeffed, I fhould have fled to meet my fatal
deftiny, have conveyed her victim to my rival, and
have now been—O ye Gods, fave me from this
horrible image!

Deterville, too generous friend! am I worthy to
be heard? Am I worthy of your pity? Forget my
injuftice:

injuftice : lament a wretch whofe efteem for you is ftill fuperior to her weaknefs for an ingrate.

LETTER XXXVI.

To the Chevalier Deterville *at* MALTA.

BY your complaining of me, Sir, I know you are ignorant of the ftate from which I am juft drawn by the cruel cares of *Celina.* How could I write to you? I thought no more. If any fentiment had remained in me, doubtlefs it would have been that of confidence in you. But environed by the fhadows of death, the blood frozen in my veins, I was a long time ignorant of my own exiftence. I forgot even my misfortunes. Why, O ye Gods, in calling me back to life, have you alfo recalled to me that fatal remembrance?

He is gone! I fhall fee him no more! He flies me! He does not love me! He has told me fo! Every thing with regard to me is at an end. He takes another wife, and honour condemns him to abandon me. It is well, cruel *Aza!* Since the fantaftic humour of *Europe* has charms for thee, why doft thou not alfo imitate the art that accompanies it.

Happy *French* women, you too are betrayed; but you long enjoy that error, which would now be my only good. I am killed by the mortal blow, while it is only preparing for you. Fatal fincerity of my nation, doft thou ceafe then to be a virtue? Courage, firmnefs, are you then crimes when occafion fo requires?

Thou haft feen me at thy feet, barbarous *Aza!* thou haft feen thofe feet bathed with my tears—and thou art fled—Horrible moment! why does not this remembrance deprive me of life?

If

If my body had not funk under the weight of my grief, *Aza* fhould not have triumphed over my weaknefs—he fhould not have gone alone I would have followed thee, ingrate, I would have feen thee, I would have died at leaft before thy eyes.

Deterville, what fatal weaknefs has removed you to fuch a diftance from me? You would have fuccoured me: what the diforder of my defpair could not have done, your reafon, capable to per-fuade, would have obtained: perhaps *Aza* might ftill have been here. But, Oh Gods!—already arrived in *Spain* at the height of his blifs!—Ufe-lefs regrets, fruitlefs defpair, boundlefs grief over-whelm me!

Seek not, Sir, to furmount the obftacles which retain you at *Malta*, in order to return hither. What would you do here? Fly a wretch who is no longer fenfible of your kindnefs, who is a tor-ment to herfelf, and wifhes only to die.

LETTER XXXVII.

TAKE courage again, too generous friend: I would not write to you till my days were in fafety, and till, lefs agitated myfelf, I could calm your inquietudes. I live: fate will have it fo, and I fubmit to the laws of deftiny.

The cares of your amiable fifter reftored my health, and fome returns of reafon have fupport-ed it. The certainty that my misfortune is with-out remedy, has done the reft. I know that *Aza* is arrived in *Spain*, and that his crime is compleat: my grief is not extinct, but the caufe of it is no longer worthy of my regret. If any regret now remains in my heart, it is due only for the pains I have

have caused you—for my error—for the wander-
ings of my reason.

Alas! in proportion as this reason enlightens me
I discover its impotence. What power has it in
a desolate soul? The excess of grief throws us
back to the weakness of childhood. As in that
first age, so in this, present objects only have
power over us; the sight seems to be the only
sense that has an intimate communication with the
soul : of this I have had woful experience.

As I recovered from the long and senseless le-
thargy, into which I was plunged by the departure of *Aza*, the first desire that nature inspired
me with, was to retire into that solitude which I
owe to your providential goodness. It was not
without difficulty that I obtained leave of *Celina* to
be conducted thither. There I found helps against
despair, which neither the world, nor friendship
itself, could ever afford me. In your sister's
house, even her conversation could never prevail
over the objects which incessantly renewed in my
mind the perfidy of *Aza*.

The door by which *Celina* brought him into my
chamber, on the day of your departure and his
arrival; the seat on which he sat; the place in
which he denounced my misery, and restored me
my letters; even the remembrance of his shadow
on the wainscot, where I had observed the propor-
tions of it; all gave every day fresh wounds to my
heart.

Here I see nothing but what recalls the agreeable
ideas I received at the first sight of the place : I
find nothing but the image of your friendship, and
that of your amiable sister.

If the remembrance of *Aza* presents itself to
my mind, it is under the same aspect which I
then beheld him. I think myself waiting for his
arrival.

arrival. I give way to this illufion as long as it
is agreeable to me: if it quits me, I have recourfe
to books, and read greedily at the firft. Infenfibly new ideas veil over the horrid truth that en-
virons me, and, at the end, give fome relaxation
to my forrow.

Shall I confefs, that the fweets of liberty fometimes prefent themfelves to my imagination, and
that I liften to them? Amufed by agreeable objects, their propriety has charms which force me
to relifh them. I confide in my own tafte, and
rely but little on my reafon. I give way to my
weakneffes, and combat thofe of my heart only by
indulging to thofe of my mind. The maladies of
the foul will not bear violent remedies.

Perhaps the faftidious decency of your nation
does not permit to one of my age that independency
and folitude in which I live: whenever *Celina*
comes to fee me, fhe at leaft endeavours to perfuade me fo; but fhe has not yet given me fufficient reafons to convince me that I am to blame.
True decency is in my heart. It is not to the
image of virtue that I pay homage, but to virtue
itfelf. Yet I will always take her for the judge
and guide of my actions. To her will I confe-
crate my life, and to friendfhip my heart. Alas!
when will it have the undivided and uninterrupted
poffeffion and fway?

LETTER XXXVIII.

To the Chevalier Deterville *at* PARIS.

IT was almoft at the fame time, Sir, that I read
the news of your departure from *Malta*, and
that of your arrival at *Paris*. Whatever the pleafure will be that I fhall tafte at feeing you again,

it

it cannot overcome my concern, occafioned by the billet you wrote to me at your arrival.

How, *Deterville*, after having taken upon you to diffemble your fentiments in all your letters, after having given me room to hope that I fhould no longer have a paffion that afflicts me to combat, do you deliver yourfelf up more than ever to its violence?

To what purpofe do you affect a deference towards me, which you contradict at the fame inftant? You afk leave to fee me, you affure me of a blind fubmiffion to my will; and yet you endeavour to convince me of fentiments the moft oppofite to fuch a fubmiffion. This gives me difpleafure, and, I affure you, I fhall never approve of fuch conduct.

But fince a falfe hope feduces you, fince you give a wrong turn to my confidence, and the ftate of my foul, it is proper I fhould tell you what are my refolutions, which are not to be fhaken, like yours.

You flatter yourfelf in vain that you fhall caufe my heart to put on new chains. The treachery of another does not difengage me from my oaths. Would to heaven it could make me forget the ingrate: but, if I could forget him, yet, true to myfelf, I would not be perjured. The cruel *Aza* abandons that which once was dear to him: his rights over me are not the lefs facred: I may be healed of my paffion, but never can have any except for him. All the fentiments that friendfhip infpires are yours, and I fhall be faithful to them. You fhall enjoy my confidence and fincerity in the fame degree, and both fhall be without bounds. All the lively and delicate fentiments, which love has difcovered in my heart, fhall turn to the advantage of friendfhip. I will let you fee, with equal

opennefs

opennefs of foul, my regret that I was not born
in *France*, and my invincible inclination towards
Aza ; how grateful it would have been to me that
I had owed to you the advantage of thinking, and
my eternal acknowledgment to him who procured
me that blefling. We will read in each others
fouls : confidence, as well as love, can give rapidity to time : there are a thoufand ways to make
friendfhip inftrueting, and banifh from it all fatiety.

You fhall teach me fome knowledge of your
arts and fciences, and, in fo doing, tafte the pleafure of fuperiority : I will make reprifal on you,
by difcovering virtues in your heart which you did
not know to be there. You fhall adorn my mind
with what may render it amufing, and enjoy the
fruit of your own work : I will endeavour to make
the native charms of fimple friendfhip agreeable to
you, and fhall find myfelf happy in fucceeding.

Celina, by dividing her love betwixt us, fhall
throw that gaiety into our converfations which
they might otherwife want. What more fhall we
have to defire ?

Your fears that folitude may be hurtful to my
health are groundlefs. Believe me, *Deterville*,
folitude is never dangerous but through idlenefs.
But I, continually employed, can ftrike out to
myfelf new pleafures from every thing that inaction would elfe render infipid.

Without fearching deep into the fecrets of nature, is not the fimple examination of its wonders
fufficient to vary and renew inceffantly occupations that are always agreeable ? Does life itfelf fuffice to acquire a flight, but interefting knowledge
of the univerfe, of what furrounds me, and of my
own exiftence ?

The pleafure of being ; that forgotten, unknown pleafure to fo many mortals ; this thought
fo

fo fweet, this happinefs fo pure, *I am, I live, I exift*; is alone enough to convey blifs, if we remember it, if we enjoy it, if we know the value of it.

Come, *Deterville*, come, and learn of me to hufband the refources of our fouls, and the benefits of nature. Renounce thofe tumultuous fentiments, the imperceptible deftroyers of our being. Come, and learn to know innocent and durable pleafures: come, and enjoy them with me. You fhall find in my heart, in my friendfhip, in my fentiments, all that is wanting to indemnify you for the lofs of love.

LETTER XXXIX.

Deterville's *Anfwer to* Zilia.

OH *Zilia!* on what conditions am I permitted to fee you again? Have you thought well on that which you require of me? I was able, it is true, to keep filence in your prefence; but that fituation was at the fame time the joy and the misfortune of my life. I could take pains for *Aza's* return; I paid a deference to your paffion for him, cruel as it was to me. Even when I fufpected his change, without given myfelf up to the flattering hopes which I might from thence have conceived, I wrought fo far upon my mind as to be afflicted, becaufe it would make you unhappy. But *Aza* came, and had a frefh view of your charms. He found you faithful, tender, wholly occupied with his idea, and your defire to crown his flame. How triumphant was it for him to fee thofe fortunate knots, the precious monuments of your tendernefs! What other heart but his would not have refumed his ancient chains? Or rather,
what

what other heart but his had been capable ever to break them?

Not being able to forefee his ingratitude, nothing remained for me but to die. I formed a defign of leaving you for ever, and flying from my country and my family: I could not, however, refufe myfelf the doleful confolation of imparting to you this refolution. *Celina*, fenfibly touch'd with my unhappy lot, took upon her to deliver to you my letter. The time fhe chofe for this, *Zilia*, as your-felf have wrote me word, was the inftant in which the faithlefs *Aza* appeared in your fight. Doubt-lefs the tender compaffion of *Celina* for an unfor-tunate brother, made her tafte a fecret pleafure in embittering the moments which were to have been fo very fweet: fhe was not deceived; you were fenfible to my defpair, and even deigned to fignify as much to me by footing expreffions, pro-per to fatisfy a heart which had no higher ambition than to engage your pity.

I was foon informed of *Aza's* crime, and then, I confefs it, my heart firft gave way to hope. The illufion prevailed on me fo far, that I even flat-tered myfelf with the glory of giving you comfort. That was the firft moment of my life wherein I prefaged to myfelf a happy futurity. To thefe fentiments, at once fo foft and fo new to me, fucceeded the moft afflicting circumftance. Your life was in danger, and my foul was torn in pieces by the fear of lofing you. I laboured ardently to furmount the obftacles which oppofed my return. At laft I overcame them; and flew towards you. My refpect impofed on me the neceffity of wait-ing for your orders to appear in your prefence. I petitioned for leave in fuch expreffions as are natu-ral to a heart in the condition of mine. But, is it poffible to exprefs what I felt upon reading your
answer?

anfwer? No, it is not poffible. How many different notions agitated my foul! how many fenfelefs
projects! That of removing from you, *Zilia*, I
had the courage to form; but, too feeble to put
it in execution, I gave way to my deftiny by remaining near you. My refpect, my admiration,
and my fervices, fhall be all that I will permit the
ardour of my love to exprefs. Shall I be forbid-
den, divine *Zilia*, to hope in filence, that you
will one day be touched with a paffion which fhall
always be as great in refpect as in vivacity?

LETTER XL.

Zilia *to* Celina.

MY dear *Celina*, how unhappy am I? You
leave me, alas! to myfelf, and I have not
a more cruel enemy. Inceffantly haunted by the
moft grievous reflections, upon misfortunes that I
could not forefee, and deftitude of experience, I
can by no means enjoy the repofe which this
charming folitude feems to offer me. It ferves
only to bring back the remembrance of the cruel
Aza, with all his charms. In vain I call reafon
to my fuccour; in vain think of my infulted love,
rewarded with ingratitude. I fee plainly, that it
is from time only I muft expect the calm I defire.
Why was it not the pleafure of love that fuch tender and delicate fentiments fhould be referved for
Deterville, who would have better known their value? But could I forefee events, of which I had
not the leaft idea? *Aza* the firft time prefented himfelf to my eyes with all poffible advantages: birth,
merit, a charming figure, and the warmeft love,
authorized by duty: what more was wanting to
engage a young heart, naturally fenfible and ten-
G   der?

der? This heart was accordingly given up without referve! I breathed only for him; my beauty was pleafing, and I defired new charms, only that I might be more worthy of him, and, if poffible, render him more amorous. Our felicity was perfect, till the fatal revolution which feparated us one from the other.

Long abfence, dependance on others, and the lofs of his riches, have doubtlefs determined him to forget me, in order to enjoy the real advantages that are offered him, and which he cannot now hope to obtain by an union with me. Befides how fhould he continue faithful to me, when he has not been fo even to his religion? One error naturally draws on another.

But I perceive, with regret, that I entertain you only on the fubject of this ungrateful man. How weak am I, my dear *Celina!* What need have I of your councils to fortify my reafon againft an unvoluntary love!—It fhall be fo.—I will make new efforts to furmount it.

Is *Deterville* at *Paris?* Has he accepted the tender friendfhip which I offered him? You two are all that remains dear to me. Come, and fweeten my folitude! Walking, reading, and reflection fhall divide our time; and I begin to think I ought to ftudy your religion. *Aza,* whofe knowledge is fublime, who, as a fon of the celeftial luminary, ought to have a more lively and penetrating wit than I, has acknowledged defects in ours, which I cannot yet fee. I may deceive myfelf in my opinion of its perfection. When I left *Peru,* I was perfuaded that was the only country favoured by the fun; that our horizon alone was enlightened by it, and that all other people were envolved in darknefs. I foon difcovered my error in this refpect. It feems probable therefore, that
the

the inſtructions which may be given me by *Deter-ville*, whoſe character is formed of rectitude, candour, moderation and generoſity may make ſome farther impreſſion upon me.

I will add this obligation to all thoſe which I already have to him; on this condition only, that he ſhall employ nothing but reaſon and ſolid proofs to perſuade me. I am willing to be in-ſtructed, but not conſtrained. This ſerious ſtudy ſhall be intermixed with innocent amuſements, which you, *Celina*, ſhall partake with us. But be ſure to make *Deterville* ſenſible, that he will crown my gratitude, if he baniſhes love entirely from our converſation. Such an union will be charming, if I hear not a word of this enemy of my repoſe. Eſteem and confidence ſhall reign betwixt us, and what would he deſire more?

Come both of you, and breathe this amiable li-berty, which is taſted in the country with per-ſons that are dear to us. You will ſupport my weakneſs with goodneſs; you will fortify my rea-ſon, and time ſhall do the reſt.

LETTER XLI.

Celina's *Anſwer to* Zilia.

I Should not have left you to yourſelf, my dear *Zilia*, if I had not imagined you more con-firmed with regard to a misfortune without remedy; I ſhould even have thought it an inſult to you, to believe that the inconſtant *Aza* ſtill occupies your heart alone. In truth he does not deſerve it. Could he be acquainted with your worth, and yet ſhake off his chains?

It is plain, that love ſtill pleads warmly for him in your heart: But does that juſtify him? You are

ingenious

ingenious in fearching out whatever may make him appear lefs culpable; that is an effect of the goodnefs of your heart, and the tendernefs you ftill bear to that ungrateful man. But my dear *Zilia*, do not deceive yourfelf: He never, in his love to you, felt any of thofe little tribulations, which warm and heighten that paffion; jealoufy, caprice, coldnefs, never entered into your engagements. Sure of your heart, he found nothing but tendernefs, and equality of humour; a paffion, perhaps too warm on your fide, and in which there was at leaft no trial. Hence arofe your misfortune; he ceafed to love you, becaufe he had been too happy. It is not eafy to decide, my dear *Zilia*, which it was that prevailed with him; whether religion, or the beauty of the fair *Spaniard*. If it was the firft motive only, he is excufable; but the two objects united together, make me very much fufpect him. You are to blame, my dear friend, to think fo inceffantly of this perfidious man: It is entertaining an idea fatal to your repofe. Let us not talk any more, I befeech you, of one fo faithlefs; let us forget, if it be poffible, his very name. I will come and fee you; I will do my utmoft to direct you. How paffionately do I wifh myfelf able to contribute to the return of your tranquillity, and the affurance of your felicity!

I reproach myfelf much for having left you alone, abandoned to your reflections; but I thought your heart cured. I doubt not but agreeable company will fweeten your folitude, and I will bring with me two of my friends, with whom I am fure you will be fatisfied.

My brother is returned, and I have fhewn him your letter. He is grieved to the heart to fee you ftill fo full of the perjured *Aza.* You owe to
                                                            his

his delicacy, and that conduct, of which he alone
is capable, the violence he puts on himself in keeping at a diftance from you. But entirely taken up
with a paffion equally tender and refpectful, he
does not find himfelf capable to fupprefs all the
teftimonies of it. He is afraid of offending you,
becaufe he is afraid that, in fpight of himfelf,
fome expreffions may efcape him in your prefence,
which you have forbid with the utmoft rigour.
He laments without ceafing, that fentiments fo
conftant, fo tender, fo delicate, to which he
thinks he has a juft title, fhould be the recompence of one that is perjured.

You offer him your friendfhip, and prefs him to
come and fee you: Is not this a real cruelty?
What! fhall he every moment behold an enchant-
ing object, for whom alone he fighs, who, by
her beauty, her fweetnefs, and a thoufand other
charms, muft enflave him more and more daily;
and yet will you have the feverity to forbid him to
fpeak of that paffion, which interefts him more
than any thing befides?

He accepts, however, with grateful acknowledgments, the tender friendfhip which you offer
him, fince more he cannot obtain. He is extremely fenfible, that this friendfhip would have a
thoufand charms for a lefs amorous heart : but for
himfelf, his paffion is too ftrong to be confined to
that fimple fentiment. Being unable to recall his
own reafon, I fee how difficult it will be for him
to fatisfy yours. Is it not, my dear *Zilia*, almoft
the want of reafon, ftill obftinately to love a perfon, who neither can, nor ought to make a fuita-
ble return for the fame?

If you defire to be enlightened with regard to
your religion, be not afraid that *Deterville* will
inftruct you with tyranny: He will give you fuch

helps

helps and such counfels, as fhall be in your choice
either to follow or reject. You know his inte-
grity and moderation: I am fure he will act under
their direction, though at the fame time it will
give him the purest joy if he can fucceed. But,
my dear *Zilia*, in order to this great work, it is
neceffary to be divefted of all prejudice.

We promife ourfelves much enjoyment of your
converfation, and will endeavour to make ours as
agreeable as we are capable. This will be eafy
for us to do, as our hearts are free from love, and
filled only with tranquil friendfhip. *Deterville*
himfelf, whom we have at laft engaged to be of
the party, has promifed me fincerely, that he will
not appear amorous, but obferve all the rules of
difcretion you prefcribe to him; but he befeeches
you, in return, never to fpeak to him of the
faithlefs and happy *Aza*. He has a right, me-
thinks, to require this complaifance of you. I
know not whether it will be very difficult to you;
but it is neceffary there fhould be an unifon betwixt your two hearts, in order to form a perfect
concert amongft us.

LETTER XLII.

Deterville *to* Celina.

AT my return from *Malta* to *Paris*, my dear
fifter, I received with a tranfport of joy,
mixed with fear, the fair *Zilia*'s letter, which was
delivered to me by your order. In fact, this letter confirms, at the very beginning of it, her defign to forget *Aza*: But O painful and cruel
tidings! it proclaims to me afrefh her refolution
never to replace him by another. She even forbids me to have the leaft idea of that nature.
What

What a mortal blow, my dear *Celina*, was this!
Have you a thorough fenfe of it? Whilft *Zilia*
could depend on the fidelity of one fo beloved,
I had no room either to hope or to complain : I
could not be ignorant, being myfelf a melancholy
proof of it, that a heart truly fmitten cannot entertain more than one love. That of *Zilia* belonged of right to the faithlefs *Aza:* but when
this fame *Aza* became faithlefs and perjured, had
not my hopes a right to revive? Yet in that very
inftant how cruelly were they deceived! Dear fifter
how hard is my fate! What is the compofition of
thefe *Peruvian* fouls? How! Is not *Zilia* fufceptible of that lively pleafure, which all women,
may I not fay, which all hearts enjoy in vengeance? Why does fhe not efface from her heart
the very image of this ingrate, if it were for no
other reafon than to fhew her horror of ingratitude! Happy, if amidft the diverfity of her fentiments, a fpark of love for me could enter. I
am fenfible that my delicacy would fuffer by thofe
means, but no matter, if fhe does but love me. I
fhall owe my happinefs to fpite; but perhaps I
may owe it to gratitude likewife. Shall I not be a
thoufand times happy? I cannot help for a moment
enjoying the idea.

It is true, that this beauty whom I adore, offers
me the moft conftant friendfhip, and expreffes it
even with paffion: fhe particularifes all the
charms of it with fo much grace and delicacy,
that if any other than *Zilia* had offered me fuch a
friendfhip, I fhould have been enchanted with it.
But can the moft tender friendfhip on her part
repay the moft paffionate love on mine? Feeble
image of a paffion, how will it anfwer to the vivacity of that which I feel! How great will be
my misfortune, if, while *Zilia* renders for the

moft

moſt tender love the ſimple ſentiment of tranquil friendſhip, her heart forgetting at laſt the faithleſs *Aza*, ſhould melt in favour of ſome other than me! I ſhudder with dread and horror at the thought. Alas! ſuch a new engagement would torment me for ever. To be always near the object in which alone my felicity conſiſts, and always far from felicity itſelf, is a ſituation, that inſtead of curing the evils I ſuffer, would ſerve only to augment them.

Pity me, my dear *Celina*, deplore ſincerely thy brother's condition, if thou haſt any idea of what love is without hope.

LETTER XLIII.

Celina *to* Deterville.

IDo indeed commiſerate a diſtracted heart, which finds no relief either in itſelf or elſewhere. Such is your ſituation, my dear *Deterville*; you love *Zilia*, the moſt amiable, the moſt virtuous virgin that ever was, and you love her almoſt without meaſure. The purity of her ſoul, the natural delicacy of her converſation, her beauty for ever new to your eyes, her candour, even her very tenderneſs for *Aza*, contrary as it is to you, hopes, all contribute to nouriſh in you a paſſion, which taſte and eſteem augment daily; a paſſion ſo much the more lively, as it is the firſt you have ever experienced. I would endeavour to cure you of it, if it were of ſuch a nature as you could ever repent it; but I am not ignorant, that being maſter of this fair *Indian*, by the laws of war, you have reſpected her beauty, her ſentiments, and her misfortunes: I know it was not your fault, that the only good, which could render
der

der her happy, was not reftored to her, and that even at the expence of your wealth. I admired you as a prodigy, when I faw you call out of the heart of *Spain* the happy *Aza*, in order to return to him, with his other treafures, the only jewel which you could not be happy without. This was the very height of generofity.

In the mean time, by an unexampled turn of fortune, when the infidelity of *Aza* rendered your benefits ufelefs, and you had more right than ever to hope, the unforefeen conftancy of *Zilia* for an ungrateful man, adds the laft and fevereft ftroke to your misfortunes.

But, my dear brother, while I indulge your grief, and lament the fatality of your ftars, fuffer me to inform you, that you make your cafe worfe than it really is. The anxiety of your heart, doubtlefs prevents your feeing the leaft glimpfe of hope : but perhaps the indifference, in which you formerly lived, keeps you ignorant of the re-fources which are ftill left you by fortune. As a woman, I fhould be tempted ftill to leave you partly in ignorance; but as a fifter, I cannot take fuch an unkind refolution. Hear me then, my dear *Deterville. Aza* was naturally the only object that *Zilia* could be attached to. A prince, tender, young and charming, and *Zilia* in all the force and fweetnefs of her firft fires, united by tafte and by duty, and by the virtue which ennobled both. A hideous mifhap, a cruel revolution fe-parates them, and enlivens the image of that fe-licity of which they fee themfelves fatally depri-ved. Reprefent to yourfelf how much force even defpair muft add to a paffion before fo warm and fo legitimate. It was a heart new in love, full of fire, given up for the firft time, and which did not know a more fenfible pleafure, than that of

G 5   adhering

adhering to the object it had chosen; in short, it was a heart amorous to excess, inflamed by difficulty, and which, at the very brink of felicity, saw itself in that instant, snatched from the expected enjoyment. My dear brother, put yourself for a moment in the place of *Zilia:* Is it possible that any other lover could make her so soon forget a bridegroom that was so dear to her, and restore her tranquillity? Reflect on the nobleness of her soul, and you will conceive that a heart so generous, may be capable of carrying her attachment beyond the bounds of ordinary sensibility, and of continuing to love an object which it is sure never to possess. This is such a musical string, as sounds a long time after it has been once briskly touched.

But do you not see, my dear *Deterville,* that this sentiment is too contrary to nature to be durable? Do you doubt whether *Zilia,* when she comes to reflect more quietly, will perceive the injustice of *Aza,* the weight of his indifference, and the inutility of loving without return? Maintained hitherto in her tenderness, by a kind of forcery, the illusion she puts on herself will soon dissipate, the image of *Aza* will in a short time become burthensome, and then her heart, void of interest and employment, will with difficulty support itself in such a state of inaction. A tiresome state of languor is an insupportable burthen for an active soul. *Zilia* will wish for some pretence to get rid of it, and what pretence will be more happy for you both, than that of gratitude? *Zilia* professes her acknowledgments to you, and is fully sensible how much she owes to your generous proceedings.

I come now to the friendship which she offers you. By your refusing this friendship, it should

seem

feem to be offenfive, or at leaft unpleafant to
you. You look upon it as a fentiment too weak
to anfwer to the vivacity of your love. It feems
like a payment in counterfeit coin ; and you rejeƈt
it becaufe it is not abfolute and complete love :
But, pray dear brother, is it the name only that
you would obtain ? For my part, I cannot help
thinking fo : for the friendfhip of *Zilia* ought to
infpire you with lefs repugnance. Let me tell
you, even this ought to charm you. Why do
you oblige me here to difclofe the great fecrets of
the fair fex ? Know, that this fentiment of friendfhip, fo fweet among men, fo rare among women, is always the moft lively betwixt perfons of
different fexes. Men love one another with cor-
diality, women love each other with diffidence ;
but two perfons of the two fexes add to the tafte
of friendfhip, a fpark of that fire which nature
never fails to infpire. A fprout of paffion will
attend the very birth of this friendfhip, fo pure
in appearance ; as fuch fort of friends are fully
enough fenfible. Let them both keep mutually
upon their guard, it matters not : All their precau-
tions will make no change in the imperceptible
progrefs of nature, and they will foon be furprized, that they are fallen in love with each other
without perceiving it.

The friendfhip offered you then, my dear *Deterville*, is, in my opinion, the firft aƈt of that
interefting play, of which you fo much defire to
fee the unravelling ; it is the firft difcovery of the
heart, and fince that is favourable to you, have
you any room to complain ?

It is true, that the name of friendfhip fpreads
a veil, which hides a part from your fight : but it
is a veil wrought by the hands of love, made only
to deceive jealous eyes, but which hides nothing
from

from eyes that can penetrate, nor long conceals the truth from him who is the object of it. Do you not now confess, my dear brother, that I had room to be surprized, when I heard you complain so bitterly of the only part that *Zilia* ought to have taken? Reflect upon it well, and you will be of my sentiment. Can there be a more happy method, a method better adapted to the delicacy of you both?

Would you not always have the better opinion of a lady, who chuses to be the more reserved, to make your happiness the more compleat? Who, by giving your passion a reasonable character, intends to refine and increase your pleasure?

Indeed, my brother, you are obliged to *Zilia*, who in the way of friendship is preparing for you pleasures more extatic than you proposed for yourself: She neither dared, nor ought to make you a return of passion in the manner that you desired. You must consult the fair sex for sentiments of this nature; and be not ashamed that the women are here beforehand with you; since without them, the men would perhaps be ignorant in the finesses of the art of love. Women are allowed, as a natural consequence of the temper of their hearts, to have more suppleness of genius than men. I do not suppose any artifice to enter into this art of of love, of which I am speaking; these two characters, as much as they resemble one another, ought to be distinguished. All the women of wit love with art, but not all with artifice. As to your dear *Zilia*, her heart is honest, noble, and elevated; but she is ingenuous in the most fine and subtle manner of any woman I know. That heart of hers, which is at present wholly taken up with the most tender and virtuous passion, but a passion cruelly deceived, you will at last find to
be

be reserved for you. Allow only a reasonable term to *Zilia* for grief, and, without complaining, leave time to destroy in her that idea of glory which flatters her hitherto.

That singular honour of remaining faithful to her first ties, even when they are broken without possibility of a reunion, is a sentiment which certainly she has not learned among us : she will therefore at last give way to our example. Being then free, fearing liberty thro' a habitude of not enjoying it, and sensible at the same time of your generous cares ; the friendship, which she now regards only as a sweet sympathy, will want but one advance farther to become love ; and that miracle will be accomplished without her perceiving it.

My dear *Deterville*, what a charming prospect lies here before you ! I thing you must see enough of it to engage you, without the least difficulty, to accept the party which *Zilia* proposes to you with so good a grace. From your solicitudes, disinterested in appearance, and more still from the nature of a female heart, expect the felicity of which you began to despair.

LETTER XLIV.

Zilia *to* Deterville.

AFTER the loss of *Aza*, I could never have thought, Sir, that new troubles would have reached my heart. But now, by fatal experience, I perceive the contrary, from a discovery I made accidentally, and which plunges me again into the most cruel perplexity. Your sister came to see me yesterday. After her departure I found a paper in my chamber. I opened it ; but how great was

my

my furprize to know 'her hand, in a letter addreffed to you, in which, after blaming you for not
accepting my offers, fhe undertakes to perfuade
you by motives very different from mine! Who
could have thought that the ever-tender, the ever-
generous *Celina*, my only confolation in the bitternefs of my foul, would have proved perfidious?
After I have given myfelf up entirely to the fweetnefs of her friendfhip, and had not the leaft referve
in my fincere love to her, I learn that fhe does not
love me without diftruft. If your fifter, at the
beginning of this fatal letter, loads me with praifes,
doubtlefs they do not flow fo much from her own
fentiments, as from her fear of difpleafing you:
For on what does fhe pretend to found your hope,
if not upon the want of folidity in thefe virtues
which fhe attributes to me? In revealing to you
the fecrets of her fex, her art, or rather artifice,
does not turn to the advantage of her heart.
Miftaken notion! does fhe think the virgins devoted to the Sun, and educated in his temple, are to
be judged of by the general diftinction fhe gives
of the character of women? Is there but one
model, one rule to form a judgment by? The
Creator, who diverfifies his works in a thoufand
manners, who imparts to every country fome
particular property, who gives to us all phyfiog-
nomics fo various and different, has he decreed
that the characters of the mind fhould be every
where alike, and that all reafonable beings fhould
think in the fame manner? For my part, I cannot eafily be perfuaded of this. Befides, what
reafon has fhe to give to the men fuch happy pre-
rogatives? Does fhe believe they have a more
ample portion of the breath of the divinity? We
have, in *Peru*, fuch an opinion of the divine
Amutas, whofe fublime knowledge and habitudes,
                                        confecrated

confecrated to virtue, elevate them above ordinary
men; but for other men, if they have paffions
which are common to them, we acknowledge in
them virtues alfo which conduct and rectify thofe
paffions; and we judge of them from their actions,
and not from any prefuppofed weakneffes.

How could fhe undertake to perfuade you, that
there was fo little firmnefs in my fentiments? Certainly fhe has not learned this from what is paffed.
My heart, formed to franknefs from my infancy,
never ftrove to perfuade the unfaithful *Aza* of the
fincerity of my fires, any other way than by the
vivacity with which they were expreffed.

I am ignorant, and would ever be ignorant of
that art, which degrades women much more than
it fets off their charms: It only proves their weaknefs, their vanity, and their diffidence of the
object they would enflave. Nature knows not
this art, nor ever ftrives to adorn the graces, and
add charms to virtue.

Vainly doth *Celina* pretend to diftinguifh art
from artifice: I am not impofed upon by that
idea. Does fhe feek for difguife when it is her
intereft to hide nothing? Could one dare to confefs, without a blufh, that one had taken great
pains to lead another into error?

I hope all from the generofity of your heart.
Worthy as you are to have been born among us,
I am fure no injurious fufpicion has yet entered
your foul; and I fhould be very forry to have you
fee this wicked letter, left it fhould induce you to
fufpect. But fhould I, *Deterville*, be worthy
your goodnefs, if the too credulous *Celina* thought
juftly?

As you are too virtuous to think I aim at glory
in performing my duty, do not expect that either
time, or the weaknefs of my fex will make any
change

change in me ? United with *Aza,* in ties which
death only fhould have diffolved, no objeƈt can
difengage me from him. Yet come, Sir, enjoy
the tranquil fruits which gratitude offers you ;
come, and at once enlighten and adorn my underftanding.

Difengaged from tumultuous paffions, you will
find that friendfhip alone is worthy to fill our hearts,
and alone able to make our deftiny perfeƈtly happy.

LETTER XLV.

Deterville *to* Zilia.

I Was fet out, adorable *Zilia,* in the firm refolution to forget you, as the only relief to
my pains I could think of. A long abfence, I
prefumed, might work this miracle. But alas!
the anger infpired by a tender fentiment is foon
ftifled by its own principle. I am here returned
more amorous and as ill treated as ever, in fpite of
the glimmerings of hope which the infidelity of
Aza had kindled in my mind. My fituation gives
me more right than ever to complain : but how
cruel foever your manner of thinking be to me,
it ftill deprives me of liberty. You bind me to
you in fo engaging a manner, by the tender
friendfhip you offer me, that though the bounds
you prefcribe to it appear to me a fpecies of ingratitude, I perceive that my complaints, fhould I
now make them, would become unjuft.

While I fubmit to the rigour of your laws, my
heart dares ftill to preferve the hope of molifying
that rigour. Pardon my diforder and my fincerity : I exprefs the fimple notions of my heart ;
I am pleafed with thefe illufions and forry when

my

my reafon returns to convince me of my rafhnefs :
then I blufh for a moment; but foon the ideas
of a happy futurity triumph.   Such is my weaknefs! a mortifying reflection for me, but a reflection that raifes fo much the more the glory of
the daughter of the Sun.

In your prefence, fair *Zilia*, one of your looks
will recall the refpect that is due to you : My ardour to pleafe you will raife me above fenfe, and
you fhall be the rule of my manners.   Bound and
united together only by the fentiments of the foul,
and fimilitude of genius, we fhall have nothing
to fear from thofe difgufts, which the anxiety of
the paffions drag along with them.   Our quiet and
unweary days, like a perpetual fpring, when all
feems to ftart frefh out of the hands of nature,
fhall flow in perfect felicity ; we fhall enjoy mutually the benefits of this nature, and crown with
it our innocence.   If we at any time fpeak of
Aza, it fhall be only to recall and complain of his
ingratitude. Perhaps deftiny alone was culpable
of his change.   But however that may be, he
was no longer worthy of the virgin of the fun,
after he had breathed the native air of the cruel
enemies of *Peru*.

Let me beg you to bear no ill will to my fifter ;
her tendernefs for me, and her fenfe of my fituation, have made her imagine all the reafons that
you have feen, in order to comfort me, and give
a new birth to my hope :   This motive ought to
be her excufe. Promife me to pardon her, divine *Zilia* : There fhould be nothing to embitter
the fweets of that charming fociety, which we
propofe to form in your company.

In this hope, I fet out to come and throw myfelf at your feet: I will look upon this new habitation as the temple of the fun : I will there
refpectfully

respectfully adore the luminary that enlightens it, and the object of all my cares shall be, to render you incessantly the most pure and most submissive homage.

LETTERS

OF

A Z A

THE

PERUVIAN.

ADVERTISEMENT.

THE reading of the Peruvian Letters made me recollect that I had seen in Spain, some years since, a collection of letters by a Peruvian, whose history has since appeared to me strongly to resemble that of Zilia. I procured that manuscript, and I found that they were the very letters of Aza, translated into Spanish. We are, doubtless, obliged to Kanhuiscap, the friend of Aza, to whom the principal part of these letters are addressed, for their translation from the Peruvian.

I found a concern for Aza excited in me by reading these letters, that engaged me to undertake their translation. I perceived with joy, those odious ideas effaced from my mind, which Zilia had given me, of a prince more unfortunate than inconstant. I imagine that others will experience the same pleasure: for to see virue justified is at all times pleasing.

There are many who will, perhaps, think it a crime in Aza, to have described, under the name of Spanish manners, those failings, and even vices, that are peculiar to the French nation. How specious soever this charge may appear, it will be easily liquidated, if we properly consider, with M. Fontenelle, that a native of England and of France are countrymen at Pekin.

I dare

I dare not flatter myfelf with having painted
in their proper colours, thofe noble images, thofe
grand and beautiful ideas, that are to be found in
the Spanifh original: I might impute it to the
difference of the two languages, and to the common lot of tranflations; the reader, perhaps, will
impute it to me; and we may both of us be right
in our fentiments.

LETTERS

OF

AZA the PERUVIAN.

LETTER I.

To Zilia.

MAY thy tears be diffipated like the dew before the rifing fun! May thy fetters, changed into flowers, fall at thy feet ! and by the vivacity of their colours exprefs the ardency of my love, more glowing than that divine luminary which gave it birth. *Zilia* difmifs thy fears—*Aza* ftill lives : that is, for ever loves thee.

Our miferies have an end. The happy moment approaches that fhall unite us for ever. O divine felicity! Why do we yet pant for thy enjoyment ?

The predictions of *Viracocha* are ftill unaccomplifhed. I am now on the auguft throne of *Manco-Capa*, and *Zilia* is not by my fide. I reign, and thou art loaded with fetters ! Be comforted, thou tender object of my ardent affections. The
fun

fun has too fully proved our love ; he now prepares to crown it with felicity. Thefe knots, the
weak interpreters of our fentiments : thefe knots,
whofe ufe I blefs, but whofe fate I envy, fhall
behold thee free. From out thy frightful prifon
thou fhalt fly to my arms. As the dove efcaped
from the talons of the vulture, flies to participate
of happinefs with her faithful companion, fo fhalt
thou repofe in my heart, yet trembling with agitation, thy paft afflictions ; thy tendernefs and my
felicity. What joy, what tranfport! To drown
thy miferies in blifs ! Thou fhalt fee at thy feet
thofe brutal mafters of the thunder : and even
thofe hands which have loaded thee with fetters,
fhall aid in feating thee on the throne.

But why fhould the remembrance of my misfortunes pollute fo pure a happinefs ? Why muft I
remind thee of miferies that are no more ? Do
we not depreciate the favours of the gods when
we neglect to enjoy them in their full extent?
Not to forget our misfortunes is in a manner to
merit them. Yet you defire my dear *Zilia*, that
I fhould add to my afflictions the difgrace of having deferved them. I love thee—I can tell it
thee—I foon again fhall behold thee ; what new
eclairciffements can I give thee of my fate ? Can
I defcribe what is paft, when I am not able to exprefs the fentiments that at this moment agitate
my foul !—But what do I fay ? *Zilia* you will
have it fo.

Remember then, if you can do it and yet live,
that day, that horrid day, whofe Aurora was refplendent with joy.

The fun, in the fulnefs of his glory, fpread
over my vifage the fame rays with which he illu-
minated thine. Tranfports of joy, and flames of
love, enrapt my heart. My foul was loft in that
divinity

divinity from whom it derives its being. My eyes
fparkled with the fires they received from thine,
and fpoke a thoufand defires. Reftrained by the
decorum of ceremonies. I went to the temple:
my heart flew thither. There I beheld thee;
more fair than the morning ftar, more blooming
than the new blown rofe ; accufing the *Cucipatas*
of delay ; and to me tenderly lamenting the ob-
ftacle by which we were yet feparated. When
in a moment, O dreadful remembrance! the
lightenings flafhed, the thunder roared. At the
tremendous alarm all around me I fell to
the earth. Proftrate I adored the fovereign *Tal-*
por. I implored for thee. The peals were redoubled—they relented—they ceafed. I rofe
trembling for thy fafety. What horror! what a
dreadful profpe£t! furrounded by a cloud of ful-
pher, by flames and by blood; in a frightful confufion, my eyes faw nothing but death ; my ears
heard nothing but fcreams ; my heart fought nothing but thee ; and every obje£t told it thou wert
loft. I ftill hear the thunder that ftruck thee :
I fee thee pale, disfigured; thy bofom fmeared
with blood and duft : a cruel fire devours thee.

The clouds difappear : the obfcurity is difperfed.
Can you believe it, *Zilia?* It was not the great
Talpor. The Gods are not fo cruel. Thofe barbarians, the ufurpers of their power, had ufed it
to our deftru£tion. No fooner did I difcover the
detefted crew, than I fprang amidft them. Love,
and the Gods whofe powers they had profaned,
lent my their aid. Thy prefence augmented it,
I bore down all before me. Yet a moment and I
had fecured thee : but they bore you through the
facred portal, and you vanifhed from my fight.
Grief feized my foul : difpair drew tears from my
eyes. Diftra£ted with rage, I darted on them.
H

They

They furrounded me. By the fury of the affault, my very arms were deftroyed. Exhaufted by the violence of my efforts, and overpowered by numbers, I fell upon the profaned bodies of my anceftors.* There my blood and my tears were ig-nominioufly fhed amidft thy expiring companions; even on thofe garlands which thy hands had woven, and with which thou fhouldft have crowned my head. A mortal coldnefs feized my fenfes. My fight grew dim, it vanifhed. I ceafed to live, but could not ceafe to love thee.

Doubtlefs it was love, and the hopes of avenging thy injuries, my dear *Zilia*, that reftored me to life. I found myfelf in my palace, furrounded by my attendants. Fury was fucceeded by defpondency: I fent forth the moft bitter lamentations. Then feized my arms, and urged my guards to vengeance. Perifh! I cried, perifh! thofe impious wretches, who have violated our moft facred afylums! arm! attack! deftroy the inhuman monfters! Nothing could calm my tranfports; till *Capa Inca*, my father, informed of my fury, af-fured me that I fhould again behold thee; that you were in fafety; and that we fhould yet enjoy each other. What new tranfport what ex-tacies then poffeffed my foul. O my dear *Zilia*, can the heart that has once known fuch pleafure ever exift without it?

A bafe avidity for a defpicable metal, was the fole motive that brought thefe barbarians to our coafts. My father knew their defigns, and has prevented their demands. No fooner fhall they have reftored thee to my vows, than they will de-part, loaded with prefents. This people whom
gold

---

* The *Peruvians* place the embalmed bodies of their kings in their temples.

gold has armed againft us, and has made our
friends, are now divefted of their ferocity, and
give us inceffant marks of their gratitude and refpect. They bow down before me, as our *Cucipatas* do before the fun. Is it poffible that a
wretched mafs of matter can thus change the heart
of man; and of barbarians, as they were, make
them the inftruments of my felicity. Is it in
the power of a metal, and of monfters, to retard, and at laft to complete our happinefs.

Adorable *Zilia!* light of my foul! what agitations has thy defcription of our direful feparation given me? I have been prefent with thee in
every danger. My fury was renewed: but the
affurances of thy love, like a potent balm, has
appeafed that wound which you gave my heart.
No, *Zilia*, life has no joy to be compared with
thy love: all my powers are loft in that paffion:
my impatience increafes every moment: it devours
me; I burn; I die.

Zilia! give me back my life. O that *Lhuama**
would lend you his wings—that the fwifteft lightning could bear you to my arms—while my heart,
yet more fwiftly, flies to meet thee.

LETTER II.

To Zilia.

DOES this earth yet exift, O *Zilia?*† Do we
ftill behold the light of the fun, while
falfhood and treafon are in his empire? Even the
virtues themfelves are banifhed from my diftracted
heart. Defpair and fury have taken their place.

H 2 Thofe

---

* The great eagle of *Peru.*
† This letter was not fent to her.

Thofe brutal *Spaniards,* who had the audacity
to load thee with fetters, but were too bafe, too
inhuman to free thee from them, have dared to
deceive me. In violation of their promifes you
are not yet reftored to me.

Yalpor, why doft thou withhold thy hand? Dart,
againft thefe perfidious wretches, deftructive
thunders, like thofe they have purloined from thee.
May fome noxious flame, after a thoufand torments, reduce them to afhes. Cruel monfters!
whofe crime the blood of thy lateft pofterity can
alone expiate.* Perfidious nation, whofe cities
fhould be laid wafte, the land fowed with ftones,
and deluged with blood. What horrors do you
join to an infamous perjury!

Already has the facred rays of the fun twice
enlightened his children, and my beloved *Zilia* is
not yet reftored to my impatient wifhes. Thofe
eyes, in which I ought to place my felicity, are at
this moment drowned in floods of grief! It is,
perhaps, through the moft bitter tears thofe fires
are darted, which ought to inflame my heart.
Thofe arms in which the gods fhould have crowned the moft ardent love, are, perhaps, at this
moment loaded with bafe fetters. O baneful
grief! O diftracting thought!

Tremble, vile mortals! The fun has lent me
his avenging powers. My injured love fhall render them ftill more deftructive.

It is by thee I fwear, thou animating fire, from
whom we have received our being, and by whom
we exift.† It is by thy pure flames, with whofe
divine

* The *Peruvians* extend the punifhment of crimes to
the defcendants of the tranfgreffor: and where any great
offence is committed, the city is treated as here defcribed.
† The *Peruvians* fuppofe the foul to be an emanation
from the fun.

divine ardor I am now poſſeſſed; O ſun! may
I never more behold thy genial rays: plunged in
horrid night, may the pleaſing Aurora never
again proclaim thy return ; if *Aza* do not deſtroy
that atrocious race who have dared to pollute
theſe ſacred regions with falſhood.   Thou my beloved *Zilia*, the unhappy object of all my tranſports, dry up thy tears.   Thou ſhalt ſoon behold
thy lover overthrow his enemies, break thy fetters, and caſt them on his foes.   Every moment
augments my fury and their puniſhment.   A cruel
joy is already in poſſeſſion of my heart.   At this
moment I ſeem to bathe in the blood of thoſe
perfidious monſters.   My rage is equal to my
love.

   I go to ſurpaſs them in barbarity : that ſhall be
my guide; I haſte to the purſuit. *Zilia*, my dear-
eſt *Zilia*, be aſſured of victory, for it is thy
wrongs I go to avenge.

L E T T E R III.

From Madrid.

To Kanhuiſcap.

WHAT divinity, ſenſible of my wrongs, generous friend, has preſerved thee to be
the comforter of my diſtreſs? Is it true then,
that in the midſt of the moſt horrid afflictions, we
can taſte ſome pleaſure ? and that how unfortunate
ſoever in ourſelves we can contribute to the happineſs of others ? Thy hands are loaded with fetters, and yet they afford me comfort : thy mind
is loſt in grief, but ſtill you diminiſh my infeli-
city.

     H 3   A ſtranger,

A stranger, and a captive, in these barbarous regions, you make me still enjoy my country, though so far distant from it. Dead to the rest of mankind, I would live alone for you. It is only to you that my distracted mind is able to express itself, and that my feeble hands can sometimes form those knots which unite us in defiance of our cruel enemies.

You will forgive me, if the most tender and ardent love does more frequently present itself than friendship and revenge. The pleasures of the one are a consolation, the violence of the other has its charms: but all things yield to love.

It is not, that subdued by the strokes of fortune, my afflictions have diminished my courage. A king, I think as as a king: though a slave, I suffer no sentiments of slavery to approach me. I thirst for vengeance, though without hope. Fain would I change both thy lot and my own. Alas! I can only deplore them.

From our native land we were transported to a new world; and in spite of my prayers, we were separated. Our friendship became an object of fear to our conquerors; accustomed to crimes, could they do otherwise than dread our virtues? Was it thus, *Karhuiscap*, that the day should have ended, on which thy courage and mine, and what is more, my love, ought to have rendered me, by victory, worthy of the power that had armed me; of that bright star which gave me birth; and worthy of thy applause: when the Sun, the foe to perjury, should have avenged his children; should have feasted them with the smoaking flesh of those detested monsters, and have drenched them with their blood?

Is it thus that I must revenge the wrongs of *Zilia?* while she, consumed by the most ardent love,

love, ftill burns in thofe fetters which I cannot
break. *Zilia!* whom the infamous ravifhers
. . . . O ye Gods, hide from me thoíe dreadful
images . . . . What do I fay, *Kanhuifcap*, the
Gods themfelves cannot banifh them from my
mind. I can no longer behold my *Zilia*; a cruel
element divides us. Perhaps her griefs—our enemies—the waves . . . . A mortal ftroke now
pierces my heart. My friend I fink under the
weight of my diftrefs. My *Quipos* falls from my
hands. *Zilia* . . . . my beloved *Zilia!*

LETTER IV.

To the fame.

FAITHFUL *Anqui*, thy *Quipos* have for a
moment fufpended my alarms, but they
cannot difperfe them. To that healing balm
which thy friendfhip fpreads over my woes, conftantly fucceeds a dreadful remembrance. At e-
very inftant I fee my *Zilia* in fetters ; the Sun dif-
graced; his temples profaned : I behold my father
bending under the weight of chains, as well as
years : I fee my country defolated. I exift by
miferies alone ; and every circumftance ferves to
increafe them. The fhades of the night prefent
me with nought but frightful images. In vain do I
feek for tranquillity in the arms of fleep ; there I
find nothing but torments. This very night *Zilia*
again prefented herfelf before me. The horrors
of death were painted on her countenance. My
name feemed to efcape from her dying lips : I
faw it traced on the *Quipos* that fell from her hands.
Unknown barbarians, their arms ftained with
blood, in the midft of flames and tumult, took
her from one of thofe enormous machines in which

we

we were tranfported. They feemed to prefent her
in triumph to their hideous chief: when, in an
inftant, the fea mounting to the clouds, offered
nothing to my fight but waves of blood, floating
carcafes, large logs of wood partly confumed, fires,
and devouring flames.

In vain would I diffipate thefe melancholy ideas;
they continually return, and fix themfelves in my
mind. Nothing alleviates my diftrefs: every thing
augments it. I hate even the air I breathe. I reproach the waves with not having fwallowed me
up. I complain to the Gods that they ftill fuffer
me to exift. If their bounty, lefs cruel, permitted me to forfake this light ; if I could difpofe of
this fpark of divinity which they have communicated to me; if it were not a horrible crime for
a mortal to deftroy the work of the divinity;
could my weaknefs be condemned, *Kanhuifcap?*
Ought my fpirit to wander in the air ? My miferies would have an end. But what do I fay?
Each day increafes them. Participate with me,
O *Kanhuifcap!* my piercing griefs: learn if it be
poffible, fome news of *Zilia*; while my diftracted
heart demands her of the Gods—of all nature—
of myfelf.

LETTER V.

To the fame.

MAY thofe divine rays which give us life, comfort thee with their moft benignant warmth.
Kanhuifcap, thou haft kindled in my heart the
moft flattering hopes. The progrefs you have
made in the *Spanifh* language has already enabled
you to learn, that the firft veffels which are expected to arrive on the coaft where you dwell,
will

will come from the empire of the Sun. By them
you will know the fate of her for whom alone I
exift. Judge therefore with what impatience I
attend your informations. I already lanch forth
into the regions of happinefs. The fituation of
Zilia is laid open to my fight. Already do I fee
her reftored to the temple of the Sun ; void of all
grief but that of my diftance from her. There
fhe decks the altars of the God, and adorns them
as much by her charms as by the works of her
hands. As fome beauteous flower after a ftorm,
but ftill agitated by the winds, receives the frefh
rays of the Sun, while the water that covers it
ferves only to augment its luftre; fo does *Zilia*
feem more blooming, and more dear to my heart.
Now fhe appears to me like the Sun after a long
obfcurity, whofe bright beams dazzle the fight,
and declare the return of a pleafing feafon. Then
I feem to be at her feet. There I experience
concern, emotion, pleafure, refpect, tendernefs,
and all thofe fentiments with which I was affected,
when in reality I enjoyed her prefence. Even
thofe, *Kanhuifcap*, with which her heart was agitated, I then prove. How ftrong are the chains
of illufion! but yet how delightful! My real
evils are deftroyed by imaginary pleafures. I behold *Zilia* happy ; and my felicity is complete.

O my dear *Kanhuifcap*, do not fruftrate a hope
in which my happinefs confifts, and which may be
deftroyed by impatience alone. Do not let the
leaft retardment, my generous friend, delay my
happinefs. May thy *Quipos*, knotted by the
hands of gladnefs, be borne to me upon the wings
of the wind : and in return for thy friendfhip,
may the moft exquifite perfumes be continually
diffufed over thy head.

LETTER VI.

To the fame.

OF what delicious waters haft thou made ufe, my dear friend, to quench that cruel fire which devoured my heart? To inquietudes that diftracted me unceafingly, and to griefs by which I was totally overwhelmed, you have made to fucceed tranquillity and joy. I foon fhall again behold my *Zilia*. O happinefs almoft unhoped for! But yet fhe is withheld from me. O cruel procraftination! In vain does my heart go forth to meet her. In vain does my whole foul attempt to mix with hers; there is ftill enough left to tell me that I am far from her.

Soon fhall I again behold her; and that delightful thought, far from calming, increafes my inquietude. Separated from my life itfelf, judge what torments I endure. At each moment I die; and recover but to defire in vain. Like the hunter who in running to quench, augments the thirft that devours him, fo does my hope render more fierce the flame that confumes me. The nearer I approach to an union with *Zilia*, the more I fear to lofe her. How often, my faithful friend has one moment already feparated us: and that cruel moment, at the height of my felicity, I ftill fear.

An element, cruel as inconftant, is the depofitory of my happinefs. Say you not, that *Zilia* abandons the empire of the fun, to come to thefe horrid climates? A long time wandering on the fea before fhe can reach thefe coafts, what dangers has fhe not to experience? And how much more have I not to fear for her? But whether does my

paffion

paſſion carry me! I am talking of miſery, when all things promiſe happineſs, joys of which the thought alone! . . . . Ah! *Kanhuiſcap*, what tranſports, what feelings hitherto unknown!—Every ſenſe ſeparately enjoys the ſame pleaſure —*Zilia* is before my eyes. I hear the tender accents of her voice. I embrace her: I die.

LETTER VII.

To the ſame.

AS ſubject to viciſſitude, as accident can prevent my felicity. *Kanhuiſcap*, ſo the term to which you refer its completion muſt neceſſarily diminiſh it.

Before the ſun can make me happy, he muſt a hundred.times enlighten the world! Before that immenſity of time, *Zilia* cannot be reſtored to me.

In vain does friendſhip endeavour to ſoften the rigours of my lot : it can by no means diveſt me of anxiety.

Alonzo, whom the unjuſt *Capa Inca* of the *Spaniards*, has appointed to ſet, with my father, on the throne of the ſun: *Alonzo*, to whom the *Spaniards* have given me in charge, in vain attempts to free me from my diſtreſs. The friendſhip which he ſhows me; the cuſtoms of his countrymen which he points out to me; the amuſements that he endeavours to procure me : the reflections to which I abandon myſelf, are not able to make me forget my misfortunes.

That piercing grief into which the ſeparation from *Zilia* had thrown me, has hitherto prevented me from giving any attention to the objects that ſurround me. I ſaw, I breathed nothing but miſery.

fery. I feemed to find pleafure, fo to fay, in my misfortunes: fcarce could I be faid to live, how then could I form reflections? But no fooner had I given to joy thofe moments that love affigned it, than I began to open my eyes. What objects then ftruck my fight! I cannot defcribe to you how much they yet furprife me. I found myfelf alone, in the midft of a world that I never thought had exifted. I there faw beings whom I refemble. We each appeared to be feized with an equal furprife: my eager looks were loft in theirs. A numberlefs people are continually agitated in the fame circle, and in which they feem to be confined. Others that are feldom feen, and who are diftinguifhed from the former by their idlenefs alone. Tumults, cries, quarrels, combats, a frightful uproar and one continued confufion. This at firft, was all that I could difcern.

At the beginning my mind embracing too many objects, could not diftinguifh any one of them. It was not long before I was fenfible of this; I therefore determined to prefcribe bounds to my obfervations, and to begin with reflecting on thofe objects that were neareft to me: the houfe of *Alonzo* therefore is become the centre of my thoughts. The *Spaniards*, I there fee feem to be fubjects fufficient to employ me for a long time; and by their difpofitions I fhall be enabled to judge of thofe of their fellow countrymen. *Alonzo*, who has dwelt a confiderable time in our country, and confequently is converfant in our language and cuftoms, aids me in the difcoveries I would make. This fincere friend, uninfected with the prejudices of his countrymen, frequently points out to me the ridiculous part of their conduct. Behold that grave man, faid he to me, the other day, who by haughty mien, his curled muftachoes,

his

his high crowned cap and numerous train, you would take for another *Huayna Capac*;* but he is a *Cucipatas*, who has sworn to our *Pachacamac* to be humble, meek, and poor. He that you saw drink those large draughts of liquors, that have left him scarce any remains of reason, is a judge who within an hour, is to decide on the lives or fortunes of a number of citizens. That man you see who is more amorous of himself, than of the lady to whom he seems to pay so much regard: he who can scarce support the heat of the weather, and of that perfumed habit which he wears: who talks with so much emotion on the least trifle: whose debaucheries have sunk his eyes, paled his visage, and even destroyed his voice; that is a general, who is to lead thirty thousand men to battle.

It is thus, *Kanhuiscap*, by the aid of *Alonzo* that I dissipate, for some moments, the anxieties that consumes me. But, alas! they soon return: for the amusements of the mind must for ever give place to the affections of the heart.

LETTER VIII.

To the same.

THE observations which *Alonzo* has enabled me to make of the characters of his countrymen, have not prevented me sometimes from reflecting on his own. Though I am an admirer of the virtues of this sincere friend, I do not forbear to remark his defects. Wise, generous, and brave, he is notwithstanding weak, and subject to those very follies he condemns. Behold that respectable

---

* The name of the great conqueror of *Peru.*

able and dreadful warrior, he faid, that firm defender of our country, that man who by a fingle
glance of his eye can make thoufands obey him :
yet he is a flave in his own houfe, and fubject to
every little caprice of his wife. So does *Alonzo*
appear to me when his daughter *Zulmira* enters.
From the imperious air fhe conftantly effects
when her father tenderly embraces her, I am convinced that *Alonzo* is, with regard to his daughter,
what the warrior is to his wife : and do not imagine that he is the only *Spaniard* who does not
fpare in others the faults of which he is himfelf
guilty. I was walking the other day in a public
garden, where I diftinguifhed among the crowd, a
little monfter, about the fize of a *Vicunna* *, his
legs were contorted like the *Amaruc* †, and his
head fo funk between his fhoulders, that fcarce
could he move it. I could not reftrain from com-
miferating the lot of this unfortunate creature,
when I was furprifed by loud peals of laughter.
I turned toward the part from whence they came :
But what was my furprife ! when I found that
they were caufed by a man, almoft as deformed
as the other, and who was pointing out to the
company, the diftortions of his brother. Is it
poffible we can be fo blind to our own faults,
when we are fo fenfible of them in others ? Does
the excefs of virtue then become a vice ?

Alonzo, though fubject to his daughter, would
be inexcufable not to love her. The vivacity of
her wit, the beauty and the graces which the
Creator has given her : her ftately port, and the
tender language of her eyes, in fpite of the fire
with which they fparkle ; convince me that fhe
has

---

* A kind of *Indian* goat.
† The adder of the *Indians*.

has a heart fenfible, but vain; that fhe is tender, but impetuous, even in the moft trifling purfuits. What a difference, my dear friend, between her and *Zilia! Zilia,* who almoft infenfible to her beauty, would hide it from every one but her conqueror: fhe who is conducted by candour and modefty, and whofe heart, the pureft and moft tender love alone poffeffes; in whom the movements of pride have no place, who defpifes all the turns of art; fhe who knows of no means to pleafe but by love; fhe who . . . . . . Ah! how fierce the flame that now confumes my heart? *Zilia!* my beloved *Zilia!* Shall I never again behold thee? What can yet retard our felicity? Are the gods themfelves jealous of the happinefs of a mortal? O my dear friend, if it be to them alone that belong the joys of love, why are we made fenfible to the power of beauty? Or why, when mafters of our hearts, do they fuffer us to afpire after a happinefs, which they are unwilling we fhould poffefs?

LETTER IX.

To the fame.

WITHOUT the affiftance of the *Spanifh* language, the reflections which *Alonzo* communicates to me could not extend beyond certain bounds, and thofe which I made myfelf could be but fuperficial. Defirous of diverting my impatience, I have fought a mafter who could inftruct me in this language. The informations he has given me, have already enabled me to profit by converfation, and to examine more nearly, the genius and tafte of a people who feem to have been created folely for the deftruction of mankind;

mankind; of whom, however, they appear to think themfelves the ornament. At firft I imagined that thefe ambitious barbarians, who employ themfelves in contriving miferies for nations of whom they are ignorant ; drank nothing but blood: beheld the fun through a thick fmoke only, and were folely employed in forging inftruments of death: for you know (as well as myfelf) that the thunder with which they fmote us, was formed by them. I expected to have found in their cities nothing but makers of thunder : foldiers exercifing in the courfe, or combat: princes ftained with the blood they had fhed, and braving, in order to enable them to fhed more, the heats of the day, the rigours of winter, fatigue, and death itfelf.

You will eafily conceive my furprife, when inftead of that theatre of blood which I had formed in my imagination, I here found the throne of mercy.

This people, who, I believe, are cruel toward us only, appear to be governed by benevolence. The inhabitants feem to be united by a clofe friendfhip. They never meet without giving marks of efteem, amity, and even refpect. Thefe fentiments fparkle in their eyes, and govern their bodies. They bow down before each other. In a word, by their continual embraces, they appear to be rather one family, happily united, than a collection of people.

Thofe warriors, who to us appeared fo formidable, are here no other than old men, who are ftill more amiable than the reft ; or youths, gay, gentle and officious to pleafe. That urbanity which governs them, that cafe with which they perform all actions, thofe pleafures which are their only ftudies, and thofe fentiments of humanity which
they

they difcover, induces me to think that they have two fouls, one for fociety, the other for war.

In fact, what a difference! You have feen them my friend, bring within our walls defolation, horror, and death. The groans of our women expiring by their wounds; the venerable age of our fathers, the piercing cries fent forth by the tender organs of our children, the majefty of our temples, the facred awe that furrounds them; all things ferved to augment their barbarity.

And now I behold them adoring thofe virtues they then deftroyed: giving honour to age; ftretching forth a benignant hand to infancy, and venerating the temples they profaned: can thefe therefore be the fame men?

LETTER X.

To the fame.

THE more I reflect on the variety of difpofitions among the *Spaniards*, the lefs able am I to determine the principle from whence they proceed. This nation feems to have but one that is general, and it is that which leads to idlenefs. There is here, however, a divinity that nearly refembles it, and this is called *Tafte*. A large felect number of adorers facrifice all things to this; even their tranquillity. There is however, a party (and that party is the moft fincere) who acknowledge that they know not who this divinity is. The others, more prefuming, give definitions of it, which are as untelligible to themfelves as to the reft of mankind. According to many, it is a divinity that is not the lefs real for being invifible. Every one ought to feel its infpirations.

ſpirations. We are to agree with the ſculpture, that it is concealed under a figure of a hideous ſhape, which appears to flutter with the two wings of a bat, and which an infant holds elegant - ly enchained with a garland of flowers. One of thoſe ſort of men whom they call here *petit maitres*, will oblige you to believe tnat this divini- ty is to be found in his waiſtcoat, and not in that of his companion, and the proof he brings (which you cannot refute) is that the button holes of his waiſtcoat are either greater or leſs than thoſe of the other.

Some days ſince I ſaw an edifice of which I had heard very unintelligible accounts. When I ap- proached it, I found at the gate two troops of *Spa- niards*, who ſeemed to be at open war with each other. I aſked of one who accompanied me, what was the cauſe of their contention. It is, he replied, a matter of great conſequence. They are about to determine the reputation of this tem- ple, and the rank it ſhall hold with poſterity. Theſe people you here ſee are connoiſſeurs. The one ſide aſſerts, that it is a mere heap of ſtones, remarkable for nothing but its enormity. The o- ther maintains that it is by no means enormous, but is conſtructed in true taſte.

Leaving theſe connoiſſeurs, I entered the temple. I had gone but a few paces, when I ſaw painted againſt the wall, the figure of a venerable old man, the ſerenity and dignity of whoſe features inſpired reſpect. He appeared to be borne upon the winds, and was ſurrounded by winged infants whoſe eyes were directed to the earth. Whom does that picture repreſent ? I ſaid : It is, replied an old *Cucipatas*, after ſeveral inclinations of his body, the repreſentation of the Lord of the uni- verſe, who by the breath of his noſtrils, produced

all

all things out of nothing. But have you examined, he cried, with precipitation, thofe precious ftones which cover this altar? He had fcarce finifhed thofe words, when the beauty of one of thofe diamonds had ftruck me. It reprefented a man whofe head was incircled with laurels. I immediately afked who the man was, that had merited a place by the fide of the Creator. It is, replied the *Cucipatas* with a fmile, the head of the moft cruel and moft defpicable prince that ever exifted. That anfwer threw me into a feries of reflections which the want of expreffions prevents me from communicating. When I had recovered from my firft aftonifhment, with refpectful fteps I was quitting the temple, when another object ftruck me. In an obfcure place I difcovered, amidft the duft, the head of an old man, who had neither the majefty nor the benignity of the other. But what was my aftonifhment, when they would have perfuaded me that it was the portrait of the fame divinity, the Creator of all things. The little refpect which the *Cucipatas* appeared to have for this head prevented me from believing it, and I came away, offended with the impofition. For in fact, what appearance is there, *Kanhuifcap*, that the fame men, in the fame place, fhould adore a God, and tread him under their feet.

This is not the only contradiction that is to be found among the *Spaniards*. Nothing is more common than thofe inconfiftencies which time produces in this country.

Why do they deftroy that palace, whofe folidity promifes at leaft another century of duration? Becaufe, they reply, it is not in tafte. When firft erected, it was confidered as a *chef-d'œuvre*, and was built at a great expence. But in thefe days it appears ridiculous.

Though

Though this nation is so much a slave to this pretended taste, yet it is not necessary that every particular person have it. There are here people of taste, who sell it dearly to those who by caprice imagine them to be in possession of it. *Alonzo* made me remark the other day one of those men who have the reputation of dressing themselves with a certain elegance, in which, according to him, they place great merit. As a contrast to that man, he showed me at the same time another who was regarded as having no taste. I am unable to decide between them, seeing the public, before whom they appear, agrees in laughing at both of them. From whence the only real difference that I can discover between him who has taste, and him who has none, is, that they both depart from nature, but by different ways; and that the God they call *Taste*, fixes his abode sometimes at the end of one of these paths, and sometimes at that of the other. Unhappy therefore is the man who takes the wrong path: he is disgraced and despised; till the God, changing his abode at the moment he least thinks of it, puts it in his power, to treat others with equal severity.

However, *Kanhuiscap*, if you will believe the *Spaniards*, nothing is more invariable than taste, and the reason of its having so often changed, is because their ancestors were ignorant of that in which it truly consists. But much I fear that the same reproach will be made by their latest posterity.

LETTER XI.

CAN I exprefs my furprize, *Kanhuifcap*, when I find that in this country, which I imagined to have been inhabited by virtue itfelf, that it is only by force that men are here virtuous. It is the fear of punifhment and of death, that alone infpire men here with thofe fentiments that I thought nature had engraved in their hearts. There are, in this country, whole volumes, which are filled with the prohibitions of vice. There is no crime fo horrid but what has here its proper punifhment affigned it ; nay, that has not an example. In fact, it was not fo much a wife precaution, as the models of vices, that have dictated the decrees by which they are prohibited. To judge by thefe laws, what crimes are there that the *Spaniards* have not committed? They have a God, and have blafphemed him ; a king and have rebelled againft him ; a faith which they have violated. They love and refpect, yet murder each other. They are friends, yet betray ; they are united by religion, yet deteft their brethren. Where then, I am continually afking myfelf, is that union which I at firft remarked among this people ? That pleafing chain by which friendfhip feemed to have united their hearts ? Can I imagine that it was formed of nothing but fear or intereft ? But what I find moft aftonifhing, is the continuance of thefe laws. What ? can a people who have violated the moft facred laws of nature, and have ftifled her voice, fuffer themfelves to be governed by the feeble voice of their anceftors ! Can this people, like their *Hamas*, open the mouth to a bit, which is offered them by a man whofe equal they have already deftroyed ! Ah ! *Kanhuifcap*, how unhappy

is

is the prince who reigns over such a people! How many snares has he to avoid? If he would preserve his authority, he must be virtuous; yet he has constantly vice before his eyes: Perjury surrounds him; Pride goes before him: Perfidy, with downcast looks, follows his footsteps; and never can he behold Truth, but by the false glare of the torch of Envy.

Such is the true picture of that throng which surrounds the prince, and which they call the court. The nearer we approach the throne, the further we recede from virtue. We there see a vile flatterer by the side of the defender of his country; a buffoon linked with the most consummate minister; Perjury escapes from its just punishment, there usurps the rank of Probity. Yet from the midst of this crowd of criminals it is, that the king pronounces justice. There it should seem as if the laws are only taught by those who are the violators. The judgment that condemns one criminal, is frequently signed by another. For how rigorous soever these laws may be, they are not made for every one. In the closet of the judge, a fine woman in tears falling at his feet; or a man who brings with him a considerable quantity of pieces of gold; easily exculpates the most atrocious criminal, while the innocent expire in tortures.

O *Kanhuiscap!* how happy are the children of the Sun, who are guided by rectitude alone! Ignorant of vice, they fear no punishment; and as Virtue is their judge, Nature is their law.

LETTER XII.

To the same.

IT rarely happens, that the firſt point of view
from which we behold any objeſt, is that
from which it appears in the trueſt light. What
difference *Kanhuiſcap*, between this people and
thoſe I thought I firſt ſaw. All their virtue is
nothing but a ſlender veil, through which we dif-
tinguiſh the features of thoſe who would ſcreen
themſelves from our view. Under the dazzling
eclat of the moſt virtuous aſtions, you may conſtantly diſcern the ſeeds of ſome vice. Like the
rays of the Sun, which, while they ſeem to give
a luſtre to the colour of the roſe, diſcover the
thorns that are hid beneath it.

An inſupportable pride is the ſource of that
amiable union with which I was at firſt ſo highly
charmed. The tender embrace, the affeſted ref-
peſt, proceed from the ſame ſource. The leaſt
inflexion of the body is here regarded as an acknowledgment that is due to rank or friendſhip.
The moſt deteſtable charaſters in the nation, and
they who have the greateſt averſion, mutually render each other this falſe homage.

A great man paſſes by you and uncovers his
head; that is an honour: he ſmiles upon you;
that is a favour. But it is not remembered, that
the purchaſe of this honourable ſalute, and of
this flattering ſmile, is attended with a thouſand
ſubmiſſions and mortifications. To ſpeak more
juſtly, in order to obtain theſe honours, it is neceſſary to become a ſlave.

Pride has ſtill another veil, and that is gravity:
that varniſh which gives an air of reaſon to the

moſt

moſt ſenſeleſs actions. He who, though poſſeſſed
of great wit and ſenſe, is regarded as a fool,
would have been held in the higheſt eſteem,
though totally deſtitude of both thoſe accompliſhments, if he had but concealed his love of pleaſure. To be wiſe is nothing; the only thing neceſſary is to appear ſo.

That man, whoſe ſagacity and accompliſhments
correſpond with the benignity of his countenance,
ſaid *Alonzo* the other day; that man of an almoſt
univerſal genius, has been excluded from the moſt
important employments, for having once laughed
inconſiderately.

You will not be ſurprized therefore, *Kanhuiſcap*
that they here perform actions in themſelves the
moſt ſottiſh, with the utmoſt ſolemnity. This affected gravity, however, makes no great impreſſion on me. I perceive the pride of him by whom
it is uſed, and the more he eſteems himſelf, the
more I deſpiſe him. Are merit and mirth by nature antipathies? No; for reaſon never ſuffers
by thoſe pleaſures which the mind alone enjoys.

LETTER XIII.

To the same.

I Cannot avoid again repeating to you, *Kanhu-iscap*, that there seems to me to be something undefinable in the character of the *Spaniards*. Every day produces some fresh contradiction. What do you think, for example, of the following? This people have a divinity whom they adore *; but far from making him any offerings, it is their God who nourishes them. You see in their temples no *Curaccas* †, as symbols of their wants. In a word, there are certain times of the day, when you would take these temples for deserted palaces.

Certain ancient women, however, remain there almost the whole day. The air of devotion which they affect, and the tears which they shed, attracted at first my regard; and the disdain with which they were treated, excited my compassion; till I was undeceived by *Alonzo*. Those women, said he, who have acquired your esteem, are but little known to you. One of those you see is paid by prostitutes, to procure them traffic for their charms.

I   That

---

* We must remember here, that it is a *Peruvian* who speaks, and one who has but a very imperfect notion of our religion.

† These *Curaccas* were statues of different metals, and in different habits, which they placed in their temples; and were a sort of *ex voto*, to express the several wants of those that offered them.

That other facrifices her fortune and her repofe to the deftruction of her family.

Unnatural mothers truft their children to thofe they would not truft a trifling jewel, in order to come here and adore a God, who, according to their own confeffion, has given them no ftronger commandment than that of properly educating thofe children.

Others, having forfaken the pleafures of the world becaufe they can no longer enjoy them, here make a virtue of depreciating vices which they have obferved in other finners.

How difficult are thefe barbarous notions, *Kanhuifcap*, to reconcile with themfelves. Their religion is not more difficult to reconcile with that of nature.

They acknowledge with us a God, the creator, who differs, it is true, from ours, as he is entirely a pure fubftance; or to fpeak more properly, an affemblage of all perfections. No limits can be prefcribed to his power; his being can fuffer no variation. Wifdom, juftice and mercy, omnipotence and immutability, compofe his effence. This God has ever exifted, and for ever will exift. Such is the definition which one of the *Cucipatas* of this empire have given me: for they are ignorant of nothing that has happened fince, nor even before the creation of the world.

It was this God who placed mankind upon the earth, as in a garden of pleafure: but they were foon plunged into an abyfs of pains and miferies; after which they were deftroyed. One man, however was exempted from this general deftruction, and repeopled the earth; with men ftill more wicked than the former. God, notwithftanding, far from punifhing them, chofe from among them

a certain

a certain number, to whom he dictated his laws, and promifed to fend his fon. But this ungrateful people, forgetting the goodnefs of God, facrificed his Son, the moft dear pledge of his paternal tendernefs. Rendered by this crime the object of God's hatred, that nation was vifited by his vengeance. Wandering inceffantly from country to country, the whole univerfe was a witnefs of their chaftifement. It was on other men, until that time lefs worthy of the divine favour, that the Son, fo long promifed, beftowed his munificence. It was for them that he inftituted new laws, which differed but in a few things from thofe that were before.

Such, my fagacious friend, was the conduct of their God towards mankind. Now, how will you reconcile this with his effence *? He is almighty and immutable. He created thefe people to make them happy ; and yet they were not rendered by any means free from the infirmities of human nature. He would have them happy, yet their laws forbid them that pleafure which he has made for them, as they for pleafure. He is juft, and does not punifh in the children thofe crimes which he has fo feverely punifhed in the fathers. He is merciful, and his clemency is not fooner exhaufted than his feverity.

Perfuaded as they are of the goodnefs, wifdom, and power of God, you will perhaps imagine, *Kanhuifcap,* that the Spaniards are faithful to his laws, and follow them with precifion : but if you think fo, your error is great. Abandoned inceffantly, and without referve, to vices prohibited by his laws, they prove, that either the juftice of

I 2   God

* We fhould ftill remember, that it is an unlearned *Peruvian* who fpeaks.

God is not fufficiently fevere ; that he does not punifh thofe actions which he forbids : or that his laws
are too rigid, as they prohibit thofe actions which his
goodnefs prevents him from punifhing.

LETTER XIV.

To the fame.

PErhaps you may have thought, my faithful
friend, that foftened by time, the impatience
which devoured my heart, began to be exhaufted.
I pardon thy error ; for I myfelf have been the caufe
of it. The reflections you have feen me give
myfelf up to, for fome time paft could not proceed, as you thought, but from a heart that was
at eafe. No longer perfift in an error that is injurious to me. Impatience frequently borrows
from a feeming tranquillity the moft cruel arms.
This I have but too much experienced. My
mind contemplated with a wandering eye, the
different objects that prefented themfelves : my
heart was not the lefs devoured by impatience.
Conftantly prefent to my fight, *Zilia* perpetua-
ted my anxiety, even in thofe moments when my
philofophy feemed to you to fecure my tranquillity.

An application to the fciences may divert, but
it can never make us forget our paffions : and even
if it had that power, what could it effect on an inclination that is founded on reafon. My love,
you know, is not one of thofe tranfient vapours,
which raifed by caprice, are foon diffipated. Reason,

fon, that taught me to know my heart, told me
that it was made for love. It was by the light of
his torch I firft perceived I loved. Could I refrain
from following his fteps? He fhowed me beauty
in the eyes of *Zilia*: he made me feel its power,
her charms, and my felicity: and far from oppo-
fing my happinefs, reafon taught me that it frequently alone confifted in the art of raifing and
preferving pleafures. You will judge then, *Kanhuifcap*, if philofophy has been able to diminifh
my love. The reflections I have made on the
Spanifh women cannot but increafe it. That
great difparity of virtue, of beauty and fentiment,
which I have remarked between them and *Zilia*,
makes me more fenfible of my mifery in being feparated from her.

That pure candour, that amiable freedom,
thofe foft tranfports in which her foul delights,
are here mere veils to cover licentioufnefs and perfidy. To conceal the moft ardent paffion, in order to difplay one that they do not feel, far from
being punifhed as a vice, is here regarded as an
accomplifhment. To attempt to pleafe any particular perfon is a crime; not to pleafe all is a
difgrace. Such are the principles of Virtue that
they here engrave on the hearts of their women.
When any one of them has the happinefs, if it
be a happinefs, to be efteemed beautiful, fhe muft
prepare to receive the homage of a crowd of a-
dorers, whofe worfhip fhe is to reward, by at
leaft one glance of the eye each day. When a
woman of this fort is what they call a coquette,
the firft ftep fhe takes is to find out among the
crowd, him who is the moft opulent. This difcovery being made, all her actions, all her arts
tend to captivate him: fhe fucceeds, and marries

I 3

him:

him: then she consults her heart. Her beauty
now is employed to another purpose; she goes
daily to the temples, and to the public places:
there, through a veil that prevents her blushes,
she regards, with a steady eye, the faithful troop
that passes before her.

Alvarez and *Pedro* soon divide her heart. She
balances between them, and decides for the former; but concealing her choice from both, leaves
them to sigh. Without discouraging *Pedro*, she
makes *Alverez* happy: grows tired of him, and
returns to *Pedro*, whom she soon abandons for a-
nother. This is not the most difficult of her en-
terprizes. She is to persuade all the world that she
loves her husband, and to convince him of his
happiness, in having a wife who scrupulously per-
forms her duty.

The public has also a duty to perform, which
it does with great punctuality; and that is to
remind the husband that he is married to a fine
woman.

These contagious examples appear to have extended even to *Zulmira*, whose heart they have infected.
I think I discover, that though yet a child, she is
possessed with the dangerous passion of desiring to
please. Every trifling action, her most indifferent
regards, have constantly something that seems to
come from the heart. Her flattering discourses,
her expressive looks, the affecting tone of her
voice, which is frequently lost in tender sighs, all
declare it. Thus it is, *Kanhuifcap*, that by different arts, Virtue here has frequently the outward
appearance of Vice, while Vice is concealed under the mask of Virtue.

L E T-

LETTER XV.

To the fame.

O That truth at which I am ftill aftonifhed! O amazing depth of knowledge! *Kanhuifcap*, the Sun, that mafterpiece of nature, the earth, the prolific fea are not Gods. A Creator different from ours has produced them; and by a fingle look he can deftroy them. From the midft of a vaft chaos, envelloped by lifelefs matter, from the bofom of confufion, he called forth the refplendent ftars, and the people who adore them. To every part of matter he gave a productive virtue. The Sun, at his voice, poured forth its light; the Moon received its rays, and tranfmitted them to us. The earth produced, and nourifhed by its juices, thofe trees, thofe animals which we adore. The fea, whom a God alone could rule, affords us fuftenance by the fifhes it contains: and man, created mafter of the univerfe, reigns over all other creatures. It was the ignorance of thofe myfteries, my dear friend, that has caufed all our misfortunes. Had we been inftructed like the *Spaniards*, in the fecrets of nature, we fhould have known, that the thunder they darted on us was nothing but a mafs of matter which is to be found in our own country: that *Yalpor* himfelf, that terrible God, is no more than a vapour which the earth produces, and whofe courfe is directed by chance: that thofe furious *Hamas*, which fly before us, we might make fubfervient to our

I 4 ufe:

ufe : had we known thefe things, could we have calmly reflected on the dignity of our anceftors, and fuffered ourfelves to ferve as a triumph to thefe barbarians !

In effect, *Kanhuifcap*, it feems as if nature ftood full expofed before their eyes. Her moft fecret actions are known to them. They difcover what is doing in the higheft heavens, and in the moft profound abyfs. It feems, moreover, as if it were no longer in the power of nature to change what they have once forefeen.

LETTER XVI.

To the fame.

COULD I have imagined, *Kanhuifcap*, that this people, who feem to enjoy the light of reafon in its higheft prefection, fhould be flaves to the opinions of their anceftors ? How falfe foever it may be, a notion once received muft here be conftantly followed : it cannot be controverted without rifk of being taxed, at leaft, with fingularity.

The judgment of nature, her voice fo diftinct, which we inceffantly hear, is drowned ; her blazing torch is extinguifhed by prejudice : a tyrant, who, though hated, is neverthelefs powerful ; a cheat, who though well known, is, notwithftanding, dangerous. This tyrant, however, might eafily be overcome, if he were not allied with one ftill more potent than himfelf ; that is, fuperftition.

superstition. It is by this false light that most
men are here guided, and which makes them
mistake fabulous accounts for real matters of fact.
A man who frequents the temples several times
a day, who appears with an hypocritical and.
distorted countenance, what vice soever he may
be a slave to, or whatever crimes he may commit, will be generally esteemed ; while the most
virtuous, if he throw off the yoke of prejudice,.
will be treated with contempt. The man void
of prejudice, is here said to be void of piety. It
is not sufficient to be what is called *wise* ; to this
must be added the title of *devote*, or else you
must expect that of profligate. The dispensers of
the public esteem, those men who are so
despicable in themselves, will never admit of an
intermediate class. To be neither devote nor a
libertine, is to them a paradox. Such a man appears to their deluded sight like an amphibious
monster.

The *Spaniards* have two divinities, one who
presides over virtue, and the other over vice. If
without affectation you content yourself with
sacrificing to the former only, you will soon be
taxed with being a worshipper of the latter. The
empire of virtue is by no means absolute ; its sub-
jects have much to fear from the divinity of vice.
They are constantly obliged to appear in public
with arms proper to encounter him, and with
which, however, they are not always able to
defend themselves. They seized, the other day,
a man who had committed many crimes, and
they publicly declared that the devil must have
led him to that excess of abomination. He had
however, about his neck a sort of cord that had
been consecrated by the *Cucipatas* of the God of

virtue.

virtue. In one hand he held another cord, on which were ftrung a number of beads, that had the power of driving away the author of his crimes; and in the other the dagger with which he had committed them.

I was yefterday carried to a fpacious place, where a prodigious number of people expreffed the higheft joy, on beholding feveral of their fellow mortals burned to death. The ftrange habits in which they were drefs'd, and that air of fatif-faction which appeared in the facrificers, as if at a triumph, made me take them for victims that thofe favages were offering to their Gods. But what was my aftonifhment, when I learned that the God of thefe barbarians beholds the fhedding of blood, not only of men, but of beafts, with abhorrence! With what horror was I feized, when I reflected that it was to the God of mercy thefe licentious priefts made thofe detefted offerings. Can thefe *Cucipatas* mean to appeafe their divinity by fuch facrifices? Muft not the expiation be even more offenfive to him than the crimes of the offenders? Ah, *Kanhuifcap*, how deplorable an error.

LETTER XVII.

To the same.

THE defire of information you appear to have, my faithful friend, at once pleafes and per- plexes me. You afk for eclairciffement; proofs of thofe difcoveries, I have imparted to you. Your doubts are excufeable: but I cannot anfwer your demands. I could have done it a fhort time fince. I conceive matters more eafily than I can defcribe them, and my mind, more docile than my hand, found evidence where it now finds only uncertain- ty. Two days fince I was convinced that the earth was round; at prefent I am perfuaded that it is flat. Of thofe two ideas my mind can form but one that is indubitable; which is, that it cannot be at the fame time both round and flat. It is fre- quently thus that error leads to evidence.

The fun turns round the earth, one of thofe men they call philofophers faid to me a few days fince. I believed it, for he convinced me that it was true. Another came and told me the contrary. I fent for the former and determined to be the judge be- tween them. By what I could learn from their difputes, it is poffible that either the one or the o- ther planet, may make the revolution * : and that
the

---

* Our author was either ignorant of this matter, or re- prefents it badly; for that the earth moves round the fun is as demonftrable to any man of common fenfe, how unlearn- ed foever you may fuppofe him to be, as that either of them move at all.

the anceftor of one of the difputants was an *Algu-afil.*

You here fee all that I have learned from my acquaintance with this rank of men, whofe fcience at firft aftonifhed me. The particular regard with which they are treated, is one of thofe things that furprize me. Is it poffible that a people fo en-lightened, can hold a fet of men in fuch high e-fteem, for having no other merit than that of thinking? Certainly they muft look upon reafon as fomething very wonderful.

A man has a fingular way of thinking ; fpeaks little ; laughs never ; reafons always ; is proud, though poor ; unable to purchafe fine cloaths, he diftinguifhes himfelf by his rags. That man is a philofopher, and has a right to be infolent.

Another, who is young, would turn philofophy into a court lady. He dreffes her in gorgeous ap-parel, and tricks her up with paint and powder : fhe is a laughing coquet, and perfumes announce her approach. They who have been ufed to judge by appearances no longer known her. The philofopher appears to them to be a fool. To fufpect him of thought would be to fuppofe that philofophy was not conftantly one and the fame thing.

Zais had the vapours, faid *Alonzo.* She muft affign a pretext for it. Philofophy appeared a plaufible one to *Zais.* She omitted nothing that might make her pafs for a philofopher. She foon began to think herfelf qualified. Caprice, mifan-thropy, and pride, juftified her right to that title. Nothing now was wanting, but to find a lover who was as fingular as herfelf. She has fucceed-ed.

Zais and her lover compofe an academy. Their caftle is an obfervatory. Though already far advanced in life, *Zais* when in her garden, is *Flora*; in her balcony fhe is *Urania*. Of her lover, awkward as well as whimfical, fhe has made a *Celadon*. What is there wanting to fo ridiculous a fcene? Spectators.

Philofophy, *Kanhuifcap*, is here lefs the art of thinking than a fingular way of thinking. All the world are philofophers. To appear to be fo, however, is not, as you fee, a very eafy matter.

L E T T E R XVIII.

To the fame.

OF all that ftrikes my wondering fight, *Kanhu-ifcap*, nothing furprifes me more, than the behaviour of the *Spaniards* toward their wives. The great care they take to conceal them under an immenfe heap of cloaths, almoft inclines me to think that they are rather ravifhers than hufands. By what other motive can they be influenced, but by a fear leaft the lawful owners fhould reclaim what they have ftolen from them? For what fhame can men find in poffeffing the gifts of love?

Thefe barbarians are ignorant of the pleafure of being feen in the company of thofe they love: of fhowing to the whole univerfe the delicacy of their choice, or the value of their conqueft: to burn in public thofe fires which were kindled in private; and to communicate to a thoufand hearts,

that

that homage due to beauty which one alone can never sufficiently pay. *Zilia!* O my dearest *Zilia!* Ye Gods, unjust and cruel! Why do you yet deprive me of her fight? My looks united with hers by tenderness and delight, should teach these unfeeling mortals, that there are no ornaments more precious than the chains of love.

I believe however that jealousy is the motive that induce the *Spaniards* so to conceal their wives; or rather that it is the perfidy of the women, that forces their husbands to this tyrrany. The conjugal oath is that which is the most readily sworn; can we then be surprised that it is so little regarded? There are every day to be seen here, two rich heirs, who unite without affection, live together without love, and separate without regret. Though this state may appear to you to be attended with little anxiety, it is, however, in itself unfortunate. To be loved by a wife is not a happiness, but it is an unhappiness to be hated by her.

Virginity, which is enjoined by their religion, is not more scrupulously regarded than conjugal fidelity, or at most it is only so in appearance. There are here, as in the city of the sun, virgins who devote themselves to the Deity. They converse with the men, however, in a familiar manner. A grate only separates them. Now the use of this separation I am not able to comprehend. For if they have strength enough to preserve their virtue in the midst of the continual intercourse they have with the men, of what use is the grate: and if love takes possession of their hearts, what a weak obstacle is such an exciting separation, which give the eyes leave to act, and the heart to speak!

A sort

A fort of *Cucipatas* are affiduous in their atten-
dance on thofe virgins, whom they call nuns; and
under pretence of infpiring them with a pure worfhip, they excite and encourage in them, thofe
fentiments of love, to which they become a prey.
Art, which appears to be banifhed from their
hearts, is not, however, from their looks and
their geftures. A certain manner which is to be
affumed with the vail, an humble mien, and a
ftudied attitude, are fufficient to employ, during
the fourth part of a year, the time, the pains, and
even the vigils, of a nun. The eyes of thefe religious are alfo more fkilful than thofe of others.
They are pictures in which we fee painted all
the fentiments of the heart. Tendernefs, innocence, languor, rage, grief, defpair and pleafure,
are all there expreffed : and if the curtain be drop-
ped over the painting for a moment, it is only to
give time to fubftitute another picture in its place.
What difference between the laft look of a religious,
and that which fucceeds it! All this artifice is, however, nothing more than the work of one man.
A *Cucipatas* has the direction of a manfion filled
with nuns; who are all defirous of pleafing him.
They become coquettes; and their director, how
dull foever he may naturally be, is forced to affume an air of coquettry; gratitude obliges him
to it. Sure to pleafe, he contrives frefh means to
make himfelf beloved; he fucceeds, and becomes,
in a manner, to be adored. You will judge by
the following inftances. I am informed that one
of thefe virgins has adorned the head of the image
of the god of the *Spaniards* with the hair of a
monk. They have alfo fhown me part of a letter wrote by a nun to father *T* . . . of which the
following is nearly the contents.

" O Jefus!

" O Jefus! my father, how unjuft you are!
" God is my witnefs that father *Ange* does not
" occupy my thoughts one moment, and far
" from being elevated by his fermon, even to an
" extacy (as you reproach me) I was during his
" whole difcourfe employed with thinking of no-
" thing but you. Yes, father, one fingle word
" from you makes more impreffion on my heart,
" on that heart which you fo little know, than all
" that father *Ange* could fay for whole years to-
" gether ; even though it were in the little par-
" lour of our Abbefs, and that he thought he
" was talking with her . . . . If my eyes feem-
" ed to fparkle, it was becaufe I was with you
" when he preached. O that you could pene-
" trate to my heart, that you might better un-
" derftand what I write to you. You came into
" the parlour likewife, and never enquired af-
" ter me. Have you forgot me then? Do you
" no longer remember that . . . You never once
" regarded me yefterday during your whole vifit.
" Will heaven fo far increafe my affliction as to
" deprive me of the confolations I receive from
" you? For mercy's fake, dear father, do not
" abandon me in that diftrefs you have now plung-
" ed me. I deferve your pity ; and if you have
" not compaffion on me, you will foon hear no
" more of the unfortuuate *Therefa*.
" You will receive from the keeper of our
" turning box an almond cake of my making.
" I have inclofed, in this letter, a billet that fif-
" ter *A——* wrote to father don *X——* I found
" means to intercept it ; and I think it will afford
" you fome entertainment. Oh! that . . . .
" The bell rings. Adieu."

After

After this, *Kanhuiſcap*, you cannot refrain from allowing that the *Spaniards* are as ridiculous in their amours, as they are remorſeleſs in their cruelties. It is only in the houſe of *Alonzo*, I believe that juſtice and reaſon prevail. I am not able to determine, however, what I ſhould think of the behaviour of *Zulmira*: it is too tender to be the effect of art alone, and too ſtudied to proceed from the heart.

LETTER XIX.

To the ſame.

TO think is a profeſſion: to know oneſelf is an accompliſhment. It is not given to every man, *Kanhuiſcap*, to read his own heart. There is a certain rank of philoſophers here, who alone have that right, or rather that of confounding this knowledge. Far from endeavouring to correct the paſſions, their only concern is to know from whence they proceed: and this ſcience, which ought to make the bad man bluſh, ſerves only to make them ſee that they have one qualification the more; which is, the unfruitful talent of knowing their own imperfections.

The metaphyſicians, for that is the name of theſe philoſophers, diſtinguiſh in man three principles; the ſoul, the mind, and the heart: and all their ſcience only tends to know from which of theſe, ſuch or ſuch an action proceeds. This diſcovery once made, their arrogance becomes inconceivable.

inconceivable. Virtue is not, fo to fpeak, any
longer made for them : they think it fufficient to
know what it is that produces it ; and frequently
refemble thofe who are difgufted with a liquor
that is excellent in itfelf, when they know that it
comes from a country that is but little efteemed.

From the fame caufe it is, that the metaphyfi-
cian, intoxicated with a fcience that he thinks
wonderful, omits no opportunity of difplaying his
knowledge. If he writes to his miftrefs, his letter
is nothing more than a precife analyfis of the mi-
nuteft faculties of his foul. His miftrefs thinks
herfelf obliged to reply in the fame ftyle ; and
they confound each other with chimerical diftinc-
tions and expreffions, which cuftom has authorized, though it has not rendered intelligible.

Your own reflections on the manners of the
Spaniards, will eafily lead you to thofe which I
have here made.

Would that my heart were free, my generous
friend! I could then paint with more force thefe
thoughts, which have here no other order than
that which my prefent agitation will allow. The
time aproaches when my miferies will have an
end. Zilia will at length appear to my impatient
fight. The thought of that pleafure diforders my
reafon. I fly to meet her. I behold her participate of my anxieties and my pleafures : the tender tears flow from our eyes. Again united after
our misfortunes . . . . How is my foul afflicted,
Kanhuifcap! in what a horrid ftate will fhe find
me! The wretched flave of a barbarian, whofe
fetters perhaps fhe bears, at the court of a
haughty conqueror. Can fhe remember her
lover ? Can fhe think that he ftill lives ? She is in
bondage ; can fhe imagine that obftacles fufficiently

ly ſtrong, have been able . . . . *Kanhuiſcap*, what ought I to expect? What lot is reſerved for me? When I was worthy of her, cruel Gods, you ſnatched her from my arms. Shall I only find her again to be a freſh witneſs of my ignominy? And thou, barbarous element, which art to reſtore me the object of my love, canſt thou reſtore me to my glory?

LETTER XX.

To the ſame.

WHAT cruel power has ſnatched me from the darkneſs of the grave? What ungenerous pity has made me again behold the deteſted light? *Kanhuiſcap*, my misfortunes increaſe with my days, and my ſtrength augments with the exceſs of my miſery . . . *Zilia* is no more! . . . O horrid deſpair! O cruel remembrance! *Zilia* is no more! and I ſtill breath! and theſe hands, which grief ſhould bind, can ſtill form thoſe knots which miſery attends, with tears bedew, and which are conveyed to thee by deſpair.

In vain has the Sun performed a third part of his courſe, ſince you pierced my heart with that moſt fatal ſtroke. In vain has deſpondency, a total dejection, poſſeſſed my ſoul even to this day. My grief, ineffectually reſtrained, has become only the more violent. I have loſt my *Zilia*. An immenſe ſpace of time ſeemed to ſeparate us; and at this moment I loſe her for ever.

The

The dreadful ftroke that fnatched her from me;
the perfidious element that furrounds her, prefent
themfelves to my diftracted fight. I fee my *Zilia*
borne on the hideous waves. . . . The fun retires
with horror behind the thickeft clouds; the fea
opens to hide its crime from that God: but it cannot conceal her from me. Through the waters I
behold the body of *Zilia*: her eyes . . . her bofom . . . a livid palenefs . . . O my friend . . .
inexorable death . . . death that flies from me . .
Ye Gods, more cruel in your indulgence than in
your punifhments! Why do you ftill fuffer me to
live ? Will you never unite thofe whom you cannot feparate ?

In vain, *Kanhuifcap,* do I call on death: he
flies from me : the barbarian is deaf to my voice,
and keeps his darts for thofe that would avoid
them.

Zilia, my beloved *Zilia,* hear my cries; behold my flowing tears; thou haft none; I only
live to fhed them : O that I could drown myfelf in
the torrent that flows from my eyes . . . why can
I not ? . . . Ah! you have none! foul of my
foul! You . . . my hands will no longer lend me
their aid . . . I fink under my affliction . . . horrid defpair . . . tears . . . love . . . a ftrange
coldnefs . . . *Zilia!* . . . *Kanhuifcap* . . . *Zilia!*
. . .

L E T T E R XXI.

To the fame.

WHAT will be your aftonifhment, *Kanhuifcap*, when thefe knots which my
hands are fcarce able to form, fhall tell you that
I ftill live. My grief, my defpair, the time that
has paffed fince you have heard from me, all muft
have convinced you that I no longer exifted. Difmifs thofe anxieties which are due to friendfhip,
efteem and misfortune; and let not my weaknefs
make you deplore my prefent exiftence : the lofs
of Zilia ought to have finifhed my being. The
Gods who fhould have pardoned me the crime of
. feeking my death, have taken from me the power
of committing it.

Subdued by grief, fcarce did I preceive the approach of death, who came at laft to put a period
to my miferies. A dangerous difeafe laid hold of
me, and would have led me to the tomb, if the
unfortunate interpofitions of *Alonzo* had not pro-
tracted my duration.

I breathe : but it is only to be a prey to the moft
cruel anxieties. In that horrid ftate I now am;
all things difguft me. The friendfhip of *Alonzo*,
the grief of *Zulmira*, their attention, their tears,
all afflict me. Alone in the midft of mankind, I
only difcern thofe that furround me, to fly from
them. May a friend lefs unfortunate, *Kanhuifcap*,
be the recompence of thy virtue ! I am too diftracted

tra&ed a lover to be a rational friend : for how can
I tafte the fweets of friendfhip, when I am oppreffed by love with the moft cruel torments.

LETTER XXII.

To the fame.

FRiendfhip, at length, has reftored me to thee,
Kanhuifcap; to myfelf. Too much concerned
at my afflictions, *Alonzo* would diffipate, or at
leaft fhare with me. With this defign he carried
me to a country-feat he has a few miles from *Madrid*.
There I found the fatisfaction of meeting with nothing that did not anfwer to the dejection of my mind.
A wood, in the neighbourhood of *Alonzo*'s villa, has
been a long time the fecret depofitory of my woes.
There I faw no objects but what were proper to
nourifh my defpondency. Frightful rocks, enormous mountains, defpoiled of their verdure;
thick ftreams flow pacing over their muddy beds;
dark pines, whofe mournful branches feem to
touch the clouds; fcorched grafs, and withered
flowers; adders and croaking ravens; were the
only witneffes of my tears.

Alonzo foon took me, regardlefs of my entrea-
ties, from thefe gloomy fcenes. It was then that
I found how much our misfortunes are alleviated
by participation; and how much I owed to the
tender cares of *Zulmira* and *Alonzo*. Where
fhall I find colours ftrong enough, *Kanhuifcap*, to
paint the grief that my unhappinefs occafioned
them ?

them? *Zulmira* the tender *Zulmira*, graced them with her tears: her affliction was but little lefs than my own. Pale and dejected, whenever ' r eyes met mine they flowed with grief; while *A n- zo* tenderly deplored my unhappy fate.

LETTER XXIII.

To the fame.

ZULMIRA, whofe cares all centred in the un-happinefs of *Aza*; *Zulmira* who participated my griefs, and trembled for my life; is now her-felf on the brink of the grave: every moment augments her dangers, and threatens her dif-folution. Yielding at laft to the tender intreaties of her father, who lay groaning at her feet, with-out hopes of affording her any relief; and perhaps ftill more influenced by the emotions of her heart, *Zulmira* fpoke. It is I, it is *Aza*, whom mif-fortune will never forfake; it is that wretch, whofe diftracted heart knows nothing but defpair; and the mafs of whofe blood is changed by love into a baneful poifon, who is the caufe of this misfortune.

It is I that have taken *Zulmira* from her father, from my friend. She loves me: fhe dies. *Alonzo* follows her. *Zilia* is no more!

I have felt for thy griefs; come and partake of mine, (faid the diftracted father to me). Come, and give me back my life, and my child. Wretch-ed man, whofe miferies I lament at the very mo-

ment

ment I entreat you to alleviate my own. Be fenfible to friendfhip; for it is yet in your power.
The moft amiable of all virtues cannot injure
your love. Come, follow me! At thefe words,
which were accompanied by deep-fetch'd fighs, he
led me to the apartment of his daughter. With
horror and dejection, I trembling entered. The
palenefs of death was fpread over her countenance:
but her darkened eyes were re-animated at the
fight of me: my prefence feemed to give new
life to the unfortunate *Zulmira.*

I die, fhe faid to me with faultering accents. I
never fhall fee you more: that is all my grief.
At leaft, *Aza,* while I yet live, fuffer me to fay
. . . . I love you. I can . . . . Yes, remember that *Zulmira* carries with her to the grave
that love which fhe could not conceal: that which
her looks, her actions have fo often declared; and
which your indifference has at laft . . . . but I
cannot reproach you: your fenfibility would have
proved your inconftancy. Devoted to another,
death alone can feparate you: it never fhall
diveft me of the love I bear you. I prefer it to
the cure of a mifery that I cherifh: Of a mifery
. . . . *Aza* . . . . She ftretched her hand toward
me; her fpirits left her; fhe fell; her eyes clofed: but while I reproached myfelf with her
death, and added my anxieties to thofe of her
defpairing father; the cares of others had brought
her back to life. Her eyes opened again, and
though ftill darkened with defpondency, fhe fixed
them on me, and expreffed the moft tender love.
Aza! Aza! fhe faid again, do not hate me. I
fell at her feet, overcome by her diftrefs. A fudden joy fhone in her countenance: but unable to
bear the various emotions her mind fuftained, fhe
again

again fainted under them. They forced me away, to save her from a repetition of such dangerous agitations.

What can you think, *Kanhuiscap*, of these new misfortunes to which I am a prey: of that misery which I cause to those to whom I owe the greatest obligations? This new grief is come to add itself to those which attended me in the gloomy desert, where love, despair, and death were my constant companions.

LETTER XXIV.

To the same.

MY friend, the lot of *Alonzo* is changed. The grief by which he was oppressed has given place to joy. *Zulmira*, ready to descend to the grave, is restored to life. It is no longer that *Zulmira* whom languor had reduced to the brink of dissolution: her eyes, reanimated, now display that beauty and those graces, with which her youth is adorned.

Though I admire her reviving charms, Can you believe it? Far from talking to me of her love, she seems, on the contrary, to be confounded by the confession that has escaped her. Her looks are cast down whenever her eyes meet mine. My pains were suspended; but, alas! how short the suspense. *Zilia*, my dearest *Zilia*, can I be diverted from my grief? Forgive those moments that I have stolen from thee: all that yet remain shall be consecrated to my misfortunes.

K   Do

Do not imagine, *Kanhuifcap*, that the fears which *Alonzo* has fhown me for *Zulmira*, can fhake my conftancy. In vain does he reprefent to me the empire of *Aza* over the heart of his daughter : the joy that our union would give him ; and the death that muft follow our feparation. I remain filent before that unhappy father. My heart, faithful to my paffion, is firm, determined for *Zilia*. No ; in vain does *Alonzo*, ready to depart for that unfortunate country, which fhall never more behold my *Zilia*, offer me that power which his unjuft king has given him over my people. It would be to acknowledge a tyrant, to avail myfelf of his power. My hands may be loaded with irons, but they fhall never enchain my heart. For ever will I entertain for the barbarous chief of the *Spaniards*, that hatred which I owe to the firft among a people who have been the caufe of all my miferies, and thofe of my unhappy country.

LETTER XXV.

To the fame.

MY eyes are opened, *Kanhuifcap :* the flames of love yield, without being extinguifh- ed, to the torch of reafon.

O immortal flames that devour my bofom ! *Zilia !* thou of whofe image nothing can deprive me : thou whom a fatal deftiny has fnatched from me for ever; be not offended, if the defire of feeking vengeance for you, excites me to betray you.

No

No longer tell me, *Kanhuifcap*, of what I owe
to my people and my father. I no longer talk of
the tyranny of the *Spaniards*. Can I forget my
misfortunes and their crimes ? They have coft me
too dear. That cruel remembrance roufes my
fury. It is done : I confent : I go to unite myfelf with *Zulmira*. *Alonzo*, I have given thee that
promife. Can it be a crime to leave *Zulmira* in
poffeffion of an error that is pleafing to her ? She
thinks that fhe triumphs over my heart. Ah !
far from undeceiving her, let her enjoy her imaginary happinefs : let her . . . . It is by this means
only that I can avenge my oppreffed people and
myfelf. No fooner fhall our union be accomplifh-
ed, than I fhall depart for the land of the Sun ;
that defolated country whofe miferies you defcribe to me. It is there that I fhall purfue
that vengeance whofe violent tranfports I now
fupprefs. It is on a perfidious people that I
will hurl my fury. Reduced to the bafe condition of a wretched flave ; and for the firft time
forced to diffemble, I go to punifh the *Spaniards*
for my deception, and for their offences ; while
the family of *Alonzo* fhall enjoy all that a grateful
heart can beftow, and all thofe homages which are
due to virtue.

LET-

LETTER XXVI.

To the same.

IF you were one of thofe men who are conducted by prejudice, I fhould imagine what would
be your furprize, when you was told by an *Inca*,
that he no longer adored the Sun. I fhould hear
you complain to that Star of the light which he
ftill afforded me ; and to thyfelf for the trouble
you took in communicating your fentiments. You
would be aftonifhed, that, perjured to my God,
friendfhip, that virtue of which the vicious have
no conception, could ftill dwell in my breaft.
But fortified againft thofe prejudices which were
taught you as virtues, you require of a *Peruvian*
nothing but the love of his country, of virtue and
of freedom. I expect from you more juft reproaches. You will perhaps, be furprized, and
with reafon, to fee me abandon a worfhip that appeared to me irrational, and at the fame time appear zealous for a religion of which I have point-
ed out to you the contradictions. I have already
made that objection to myfelf ; but it prefently
vanifhed, when I was informed that the law which
I have had the audacity to cenfure, was dictated
by that God who was the author of our being !
In fact, of what confequence is the particular form
of any worfhip, provided it be enjoined by him to
whom it is rendered. On this principle it is, that
I do not blufh to conform to thofe ceremonies which
I have formerly condemned. How great, how
awful are the works of the Supreme Being ! Could
you

you read, *Kanhuiſcap*, thoſe divine books that have
been communicated to me, what wiſdom, what
power, what immenſity, would you there diſcover!
You would there readily diſcern the hand of the
Divinity. Thoſe unſurmountable contradictions
which I at firſt found in the diſpenſations of that
power, are here evidently juſtified. It is not the
ſame, however, with regard to the conduct of
theſe men towards their God.

Do not imagine, credulous as we commonly
are, I wrote you this upon the report of a prieſt
only. I have too much experienced the falſhood
of our *Cucipatas*, to credit the fables of thoſe who
reſemble them.

The high rank which they hold among all nations, induces them to practice deceit; for their
grandeur is frequently founded on nothing but the
errors of ambitious people: it would be too dear
a purchaſe for them, if the empire of the world
was to be obtained by Virtue only: they are much
better pleaſed to obtain it by impoſture.

LETTER XXVII.

To the ſame.

IT is done, *Kanhuiſcap*: *Zulmira* now attends
me. I go to the altar. You ſee me already
there: but do you ſee the remorſe that attends
me! Do you behold the altars tremble at the ſight
of a perjurer? The ſhade of *Zilia*, bloody, and
indignant, enlightens theſe nuptials with a mournful torch; and with a reproaching tone ſhe ſays,
"Is

" Is this the faith that you have fworn to me?
" Perfidious! Is this the love that fhould reani-
" mate my afhes? You love me, you fay, and
" yet you give your hand to *Zulmira*. You love
" me, traitor, and yet you give to another that
" bleffing which I could never enjoy! Did I yet
" live . . . . ." What tortures, *Kanhuifcap*,
rend my breaft? I bear the injured *Zulmira* demand a heart to which fhe has a lawful right. I
behold my father and my people bending under a
cruel yoke, and calling on me to be their deliverer.
I then remember my promife . . . . . I go to ful-
fil it.

LETTER XXVIII.

To the fame.

*Z*ILIA ftill lives! Where can I find a meffenger
fwift enough to communicate to you the
excefs of my joy? *Kanhuifcap*, you who have felt
my griefs, participate of the tranfports of my
foul. O that the flames which now glow in my
breaft, could fly and impart to thine the overflowings of my felicity.

The fea; our enemies; death; no, nothing has
taken from me the object of my love. She lives!
fhe loves me! think then what are my tranfports!
Brought into a neighbouring ftate, into *France*,
Zilia has experienced no misfortune but that of
our feparation, and of the incertainty of my
ftate. How do the Gods protect the virtuous!
A generous *Frenchman* has delivered her from the
barbarity of the *Spaniards*.

All

All things were ready to unite me with *Zulmira*;
I was going, O ye Gods! . . . . when I heard
that *Zilia* still lived, and that she would shortly
be with me. No obstacle can keep her from me.
I shall again behold her. From her lips shall I
hear those tender sentiments, which her hands
have traced; and at her feet I shall . . . . . O
Heavens, I tremble at the thought of that which
is the cause of all my joy. My happiness confounds me. *Zilia* is coming into the midst of her
enemies! New dangers! . . . . . She shall not
come. I will fly to prevent her. What can hinder me? The Gods have disengaged me from
Alonzo and *Zulmira*. *Zilia* still lives. I receive her
from the hands of virtue. In vain did gratitude,
esteem, and friendship, espouse the cause of *Deterville* her deliver; she opposed to them our love,
and obliged them to yield to our flames. Glorious
combat! How do I admire that effort! *Deterville* stifles his love: he forgets the rights which
he had over her: And behold his generosity; he
unites us for ever.

Zilia! Zilia! I go to drink deep of felicity.
I fly to meet her, to behold her, and to die with
pleasure at her feet.

LETTER XXIX.

To the same.

YOU must accuse *Zilia* only, dear friend, for
my silence. I have seen her; and I have
seen nothing but her. Do not expect that I should

express

exprefs to you thofe tranfports, thofe ravifhing
delights in which I was abforbed the firft moment
fhe appeared to my fight. To conceive them it
were neceffary to love *Zilia* as I love her.

Muft torments yet unknown invade a felicity
fo pure ? Between the bofom of pleafure and the
den of grief is there then no interval ? After
fuch voluptuous delights, a thoufand tortures tear
my heart. My tendernefs is odious to me ; and
at the moment that I would not love, I am poffeffed with all its fury.

I have born the grief that the lofs of *Zilia* occafioned; I cannot bear that which I now feel.
She loves me no more . . . . . . O diftra&ing
thought ! When I behold her, love pours into my
foul, with one hand pleafure, and with the other
torture.

In the firft tranfports of a happinefs fo pure,
that I cannot exprefs to you the fweetnefs which
attended it, *Zilia* ftole from my arms to read a
letter, which was given her by the young perfon
who had condu&ed me hither. Difordered, af-
fli&ed, melted, thofe tears which fhe had juft
given to joy, no longer flowed but for grief. She
bathed that fatal letter with her tears. Her grief
made me anxious for her welfare. The ingrate
tafted pleafures. The grief of which I had partaken was the triumph of my rival. *Deterville*,
that deliverer, whofe praife the letters of *Zilia* had
fo frequently repeated, had wrote that. It was
di&ated by the moft lively paffion. By retiring
from *Zilia*, after having given her up to his rival,
he had completed his own generofity and her affliction. She explained to me with vivacity, expreffions that were more than acknowledgments. She
forced me to admire thofe virtues, which at that

cruel

cruel moment gave me mortal wounds. My grief then fought aid from a determined indifference. I soon abfented myfelf from *Zilia*. Filled with defpair, from which nothing can deliver me, every reflection that I make is a new mifery. It takes from me my hope, my comfort. I have loft the heart of *Zilia*. That heart .... I cannot bear the thought. My rival will be happy! Ah! It is too much to think that he deferves that happinefs.

Frightful jealoufy? Thy cruel ferpents have ftolen upon my heart. A thoufand fears : Black fufpicions .... *Zilia*, her virtues, her tendernefs, her beauty: My injuftice perhaps ; all agitate, all torment me. I am loft. It is in vain that my grief conceals itfelf under an apparent tranquillity. Fain would I fpeak, complain, accufe, and yet I am filent. What can I fay to *Zilia*? Can I reproach her with having infpired *Deterville* with a love that proceeds from virtue? She does not enjoy his tendernefs. But why heap on him thofe praifes? Why inceffantly repeating his eulogy? . . . . . Love, thou fource of my pleafures, oughteft thou to be that of my miferies.

LETTER XXX.

To the fame.

WHERE am I, *Kanhuifcap*? By what torments am I followed? My brain burns with the moft cruel fury. *Zilia*, perfidious *Zilia*,

K 5   pale

pale and dejected, laments the abfence of my rival. *Deterville* by flying has gained the victory. Heavens! On whom fhall my rage fall! He is beloved, *Kanhuifcap*, all things tell it me. The inhuman does not attempt to conceal her infidelity. Precious remains of innocence; tho' fhe knows her crime, fhe detefts hypocrify. I read her perjury in her eyes. Her lips even dare to avow it, by repeating inceffantly the name that I abhor. Whither fhall I fly? When prefent with *Zilia* I fuffer frightful torments, and abfent from her I die.

When, feduced by the fweetnefs of her looks, fhe fpreads for an inftant tranquillity over my mind, I thing fhe loves me. That thought throws me into a rapture that deprives me of reafon. I recover myfelf, and would fpeak. I begin; break off; am filent. The fentiments that by turns poffefs my heart, trouble and confound me. I am unable to exprefs myfelf. A fatal remembrance; *Deterville*; a figh from *Zilia* reanimate thofe tranfports which in vain I would calm. Even the fhades of night cannot fcreen from their violence. If for a moment I give myfelf up to fleep, the unfaithful *Zilia* fnatches me from it. I fee *Deterville* at her feet; fhe hears him with pleafure. Frighted fleep flies far from me. The day offers me frefh griefs. For ever devoted to the fury of jealoufy, his fires have even dried up my tears. *Zilia! Zilia!* How great the evils that fpring from fo much love? I adore thee? I offend thee: O Heaven! I lofe thee!

LETTER XXXI.

To the same.

ZILIA, love, *Deterville*, fatal jealousy! What distraction! A cloud hides from me the names I trace. *Kanhuiscap*, I no longer know myself: In the fury of the blackest jealousy, I have armed myself with darts, with which I have pierced the heart of *Zilia*. She had wrote to *Deterville*; the letter was still in her hand. A fatal moment disordered my reason. I formed the most rash project .... My promise, the religion I have embraced, all things prompted me. The most trifling pretences appeared to me to be as laws of equity, for {deserting her. I have pronounced the inhuman sentence. Cruel adieus .... What a moment .... Could I do it? Yes, *Kanhuiscap*, I fled from *Zilia*. *Zilia* at my feet with groans, to which mine was just ready to reply .... *Deterville!* What a remembrance! Possessed with fury I flew from her arms. But soon, vainly persisting, I would return to them: all things oppose: I dare not resist.. Gods! What have I done? How shameful is the distress! How horrible the repentance!

LETTER XXXII.

To the fame.

CEASE to wonder at my long filence: Could the cruel ftate of my heart permit me to inform you fooner of my ftate? Do not think, that diftracted by remorfe, I ftill reproach myfelf with unjuft fufpicions. It is *Zilia*, it is her cruel heart, and not mine, that they ought to devour. Yes, *Kanhuifcap*, her fighs, her tears, and groans, were nothing but effects of fhame : traces that virtue, when flying from us, ftill leaves in our hearts. It is to efface them that fhe cruelly refufes to fee me again. Her obftinacy has forced me to a diftance from her. Retired to the extremity of the fame city, unknown to any one, totally devoted to grief and misfortunes, I labour to forget the ingrate I adore. Ufelefs cares! Love in our defpite fteals into our hearts, and in our defpite there he cruelly dwells. In vain would I drive him thence. Jealoufy there fupports him : and when I would banifh jealoufy, love keeps him there. The wretched fport of thefe two paffions, my foul is divided between tendernefs and rage. Sometimes I reproach my fufpicions, and fometimes my love. Can I be charmed with an ungrateful woman ? Can I forget her whom I adore ? But whatever may be my love for her, nothing can excufe her.
Would

Would she had hated me! We can pardon hatred but never perfidy.

The solicitude and friendship of *Alonzo* have discovered that retreat, where grief, and all the destructive evils to which human nature is subject, has driven me. *Zulmira* loads me with reproaches. I have just received her letter. In her eyes I appear as an ungrateful wretch, whom neither promises nor tears can recall. I have only freed her from the arms of death to deliver her to more cruel torments. She will come, she says, and signalise in *France* her fury and my perfidy; avenge her father and her love. Every word of her letter is a dart that pierces my bosom. I know too well the powers of despair not to fear the effects. *Zilia* is the unfortunate object of her rage. Bathed in her blood it is, that *Zulmira* will appear before me. Avenging gods! is it thus that you leave to crimes the care of their punishments?

Hold, *Zulmira*, on me pour all your fury. Let the apostate enjoy a life of which remorse will be the chastisement. Thus will you indeed signalize your vengeance.

But O heavens! *Zilia* in the arms of a rival. I groan, wretch that I am, and tremble for her, while the ingrate is betraying me. Oppressed by the weight of evils, my body sinks under its weakness; while the perfidious, triumphing even over her remorse, recalls my rival. Wretch that I am! I breathe .... I still exist! But what misery to exist when we only live to suffer.

LETTER XXXIII.

To the fame.

WHAT have I faid? What horror furrounds
me? Learn my fhame, *Kanhuifcap*, and
if it can be, my remorfe, before you know my
crime. Odious to myfelf, I will now expofe it
to your fight. Ceafe to lament my misfortunes;
and make them complete by your hatred.

Zilia is void of all guilt. To reflect on it is
even an injury to her.

You know my fufpicions; their injuftice will
tell you my mifery, which can never have an end:
fomething unlooked for will for ever arife. After
the perfidy of *Zilia*, could you have thought that
heaven would have given me over to new torments? Could you have thought that her innocence, which ought to make me happy, would
have been to me the fource of the moft bitter
torments? To what errors have I been a prey!
What clouds have obfcured my reafon? *Zilia*
could deceive me! I could think it! She will fee
me no more. My remembrance is odious to her.
She loved me too much, not to hate me. Abandoned to my horrid mifery, friendfhip, confidence,
nothing can alleviate my miferies. They will
poifon

poifon thy heart with their venom, and mine will
yet find no relief.

In vain does *Zulmira*, divefted of her fury,
tell me that fhe has offered it as a facrifice to my
repofe and felicity. Retired to a houfe of virgins,
fhe has confecrated to her God, and to my happinefs, her life, and the flower of her days.

Zulmira, generous *Zulmira*, canft thou renounce
thy vengeance? Ah! if thy heart were cruel,
what pleafure would it find in my horrid miferies!

It is then only to myfelf, to the bafenefs of my
fentiments, that I owe the misfortunes which I
endure. Nothing was wanting to make me com-
pletely miferable, but to be myfelf the caufe of
it; and behold I am. *Zilia* loved me; I faw it;
my happinefs was fure. Her tendernefs! her fentiments! my felicity! ought they to have been
facrificed to a bafe fufpicion? O frightful defpair!
I fled from *Zilia*. It was I . . . Generous friend,
can you conceive the ftate in which I now am?
Can I conceive it myfelf? Remorfe, love, defpair, contend for my heart, that they may devour it.

LETTER XXXIV.

To Zilia.

THE dread of difpleafing you ftill keeps in my trembling hands the knots which I form. Thofe knots which were once confolation and joy to you, *Zilia*, are now twined by grief and defpair.

Do not imagine that I would conceal my crime from your eyes. Diftracted with anxiety for having believed you unfaithful, how fhould I prefume to juftify it? But am I not fufficiently punifhed? What remorfe! . . . . The remorfe of a lover who adores you. Ah! you would hate me! Have I not rather merited your contempt than your hatred?

Reflect for a moment on all my misfortunes. Barbarians fnatched thee from my love, at the moment it fhould have been crowned with fuccefs. Armed for thy defence, I fell, and was loaded with their bafe fetters. Carried to their country, the waves on which we floated, fupported for a time, it is true, all my hopes. I lived only by them. My heart went with you. Thy ravifhers being fwallowed up by the fea, plunged me into the moft cruel error. That which I thought had deftroyed thee, could not deftroy my love. Grief augmented my paffion. I would

have

have died to follow thee. I only lived to avenge thee. All things I effayed. Even my very oaths I would have facrificed, and have united myfelf, in defiance of a thoufand remorfes, with a *Spanifh* woman, and have purchafed at that price, my liberty and my vengeance. When on a fudden, O unhoped for felicity! I learned that you lived, and that you ftill loved me. O too pleafing remembrance! I flew to thee; to happinefs the moft pure, the moft extatic . . . . Ah! vain hope: cruel reverfe! Scarce had I enjoyed the firft tranfports with which thy fight infpired me, than a fatal poifon, of which thy heart is too pure to know the pangs; jealoufy feized my foul: his moft rancorous ferpents have devoured my heart; that heart which was only formed for the love of thee.

The moft amiable of virtues, gratitude, was the object of my fufpicions. That which you owed to *Deterville*, I thought he had obtained: that your virtue had been confounded with your duty. I thought . . . It was thefe fatal ideas that troubled our firft tranfports. You was unable, even in the bofom of love, to forget friendfhip. I forgot virtue. The eulogies of *Deterville*; his letter; the fentiments it expreffed: the concern it gave you: the grief you fhewed for the lofs of your deliverer; all thefe I attributed to the fentiment that I felt, and that I ftill feel, to love.

I concealed in my bofom the fires that confumed it. What was the confequence? From fufpicion I foon paffed to a certainty of your perfidy. I meditated even a punifhment for it. I would not employ reproaches: I did not think you worthy of them. I will not endeavour to conceal
my

my crimes from you ; truth is even as dear to me as my love.

I would return to *Spain*, to perform a promise to which my former oath had engaged me. Repentance soon followed that rage which had declared to you my crime. I vainly endeavoured to undeceive you, with regard to a resolution that love had deſtroyed almoſt as soon as it was formed. Thy determination not to ſee me relumined my fury. Again given up to jealouſy ; I fled from you : but far from going to *Madrid* to conſummate a crime that my ſoul deteſted ; though you was induced to believe it : ſinking under the weight of my misfortunes, I ſought in ſolitude, in an eſtrangement with mankind, that peace which tranquillity of mind alone can afford. Overcome by my diſtreſs, the powers of life forſook me. A long time abſent from thee, ſhall I, in ſpite of myſelf, avow it to thee, *Zilia?* All my falcuties were exerted in reviling thee. I thought I ſaw you, pleaſed with my flight, recall my rival. I thought I ſaw . . . . . Alas ! you know my offence ; but you do not know my puniſhment ; it even ſurpaſſes my crime. Ah *Zilia*, if the exceſs of love could effect it : no, I can no more be guilty. Do not imagine that I intend to move thy pity ; that were too little for my tenderneſs. *Zilia,* give me back your love, or give me nothing.

Liſten to the love that ought ſtill to ſpeak in thy heart : ſuffer me in thy preſence again to relumine that fire which thy juſt reſentment has extinguiſhed. Some ſpark may yet be found in the aſhes of that love which you once nouriſhed for *Aza.*

Zilia! Zilia! thou director of my fate ; I have confeſſed to thee my crime. If thy pardon doth
not

not efface it, it muſt ſtill be puniſhed. My death
ſhall be the chaſtiſement. Too happy, inexorable ! if at leaſt I can expire at thy feet !

LETTER XXXV. and laſt.

To Kanhuiſcap.

WOULD that by ſtriking thy mind with ſurprize, I could communicate to thy heart
that joy with which mine now pants. O happineſs ! O tranſport ! *Kanhuiſcap,* *Zilia* has given
me up her heart. She loves me. Roving in the
raviſhments of my love, I ſhed at her feet the
moſt tender tears. Her looks, her ſighs, her tranſports, are the only interpreters of our love and
our felicity.

Imagine, if you can, our joys : that moment
conſtantly preſents to my ſight ; that moment...
No, ſuch love, anguiſh, and delight, are not to be
expreſſed by words.

Her eyes, her animated countenance, told me
her love, her anger, my ſhame ... She turned
pale. Faint, and ſpeechleſs, ſhe ſunk into my
arms. But as the flames excited by the winds, ſo
my heart, agitated by fear, burnt with greater
violence. My head reclining on her boſom, I
breathed that fire of love which animated her life,
and united it with mine. She died and inſtantly
revived .... *Zilia,* my beloved *Zilia !* Into
what

what intoxicating pleafures haft thou plunged the happy *Aza!* No, *Kanhuifcap,* you can never conceive our happinefs; come and bear witnefs to it. Nothing fhould be wanting to my felicity. The *Frenchman* who delivers you this letter will bring you hither. You will then behold my *Zilia.* My felicity will every moment increafe.

The ftory of our prefent happinefs, as well as that of our paft misfortunes (far be they removed from us) has reached even to the throne. The generous monarch of the *French* nation, has ordered certain fhips that are going to encounter with the *Spaniards* in our feas, to carry us to *Guitto.* We foon again fhall fee our native land; that mournful country fo dear to our defires: thofe abodes, O *Zilia!* where fprang our firft delights, thy fighs and mine. May they be witneffes! may they celebrate! may they augment! if it be poffible, our prefent felicity . . . But I go to *Zilia.*

My dear friend, love cannot make me forget friendfhip, but friendfhip keeps me too long from love. Thofe delightful tranfports that ravifh my foul, it is in thy enjoyments that I have again found life . . . I am loft in the excefs of happinefs; in extatic blifs! *Zilia* is again my own; fhe waits my coming: I fly to her arms!

FINIS.

www.ingramcontent.com/pod-product-compliance
Lightning Source LLC
Chambersburg PA
CBHW030311270326
41926CB00010B/1325